**Eventdesign Jahrbuch**
Event Design Yearbook
**2013 / 2014**

# Eventdesign Jahrbuch
## Event Design Yearbook

### 2013 / 2014

avedition

# Inhalt
# Contents

# CORPORATE EVENT

# Audi A3 Dealer Meeting 2012

## SCHMIDHUBER, KMS BLACKSPACE, HAGEN INVENT

Location: Several locations in Copenhagen, Denmark, and South Sweden

Unter dem Motto „Way ahead" erlebten rund 3.500 Händler und Importeure aus 80 Ländern im Sommer 2012 die Präsentation der neuen Audi-A3-Familie. Das dreiwöchige Event verband vier Locations in Kopenhagen und Südschweden zu einem Audi-Markenraum.

Under the motto "Way ahead" some 3,500 dealers and importers from 80 countries were shown the new Audi A3 family in the summer of 2012. In a three-week event, four locations in Copenhagen and southern Sweden were united into a space for showcasing the Audi brand.

Als zukunftsorientierte Lifestyle- und Designmetropole war Kopenhagen, die „Grüne Hauptstadt Europas 2014", die perfekte Destination, um den Händlern die Zukunftstechnologien und Visionen der Marke Audi zu präsentieren. Das Event startete mit einer Erlebnisfahrt im Audi A3 am Flughafen Kopenhagen, wo die Gäste in der „Welcome Lounge" empfangen wurden. Von dort aus ging es zum Sturup Raceway, um auf der modernsten Rennstrecke Skandinaviens von der Sportlichkeit der Audi-Modelle zu überzeugen.

As a forward-looking lifestyle and design metropolis Copenhagen, the "European Green Capital 2014", was the perfect destination for presenting the future technologies and visions of the Audi brand to dealers. The event started with a driving experience in the Audi A3 at Copenhagen airport, where guests were received in the "Welcome Lounge". They continued from there to the Sturup Raceway, Scandinavia's most modern racing track, to experience the sportiness of the Audi models.

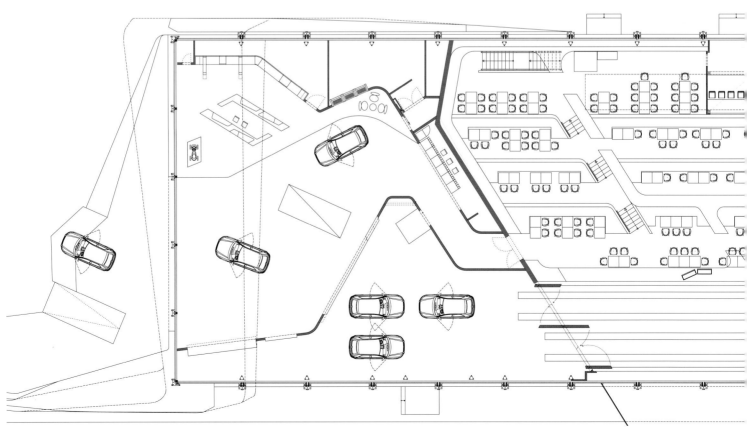

Bei einer Besichtigungstour durch Kopenhagen am nächsten Tag konnten die Gäste E-Bikes sowie den Audi A6 Hybrid Probe fahren und sich somit mit dem Audi-Markenversprechen „Vorsprung durch Technik" bezüglich Zukunftsfragen auseinandersetzen.

Zentraler Veranstaltungsort war der 2.000 m² große „Audi Pier" an der Kvaesthusmole in Kopenhagen.

On a tour of Copenhagen the next day guests could try out e-bikes and test drive the Audi A6 Hybrid enabling them to address future issues by experiencing first-hand the Audi brand claim "Vorsprung durch Technik" (advancement through technology).

The main location was the 2,000 m² large "Audi Pier" on the Kvaesthus mole in Copenhagen.

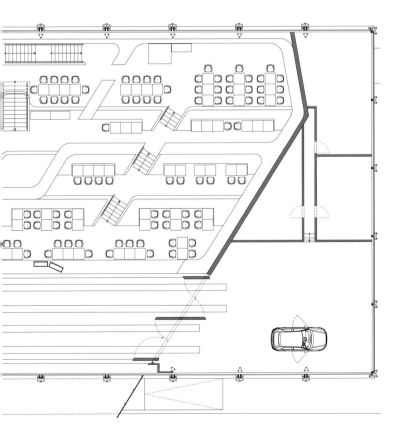

Neben einem Shop und einem Ausstellungsbereich beherbergte der „Audi Pier" ein Auditorium mit Showbühne für die Abendveranstaltung und künstlerische Inszenierung. Auf der 30 m breiten Bühne wurden die einzelnen Vertreter der A3-Familie in einer medialen Choreografie präsentiert. Dabei orientierte sich die tänzerische, musikalische und audiovisuelle Inszenierung am jeweiligen Charater des Fahrzeugs.

Apart from a shop and exhibition area the "Audi Pier" also housed an auditorium with stage for the evening event and artistic presentations and performances. On the 30 m wide stage the individual members of the A3 family were showcased in a medial choreography with musical, audio-visual and dance presentations inspired by the respective character of the vehicle.

**Agency** SCHMIDHUBER, Munich; KMS BLACKSPACE, Munich; HAGEN INVENT, Düsseldorf **Client** AUDI AG, Ingolstadt **Location** Several locations in Copenhagen, Denmark, and South Sweden **Month/Year** July–August 2012 **Duration** Three weeks **Concept/Architecture** SCHMIDHUBER **Show concept/Dramaturgy/Media display of pier** KMS BLACKSPACE **Location scouting/Event coordination** HAGEN INVENT **Graphics** TISCH 13, Munich **Construction** Ambrosius Messebau, Frankfurt am Main **Photos** Andreas Keller, Altdorf

# Hennessy XO Exclusive Collection V Worldwide Launch
## Apax Group

Location: Reed Flute Cave, Guilin, China

Für die Präsentation der sechsten Edition der Hennessy Exclusive Collection orientierte sich die Konzeption des Events am Erscheinungsbild des Produktes. Die Cognac-Flasche, deren Verpackung dem Aussehen eines Felsbrockens nachempfunden ist, bestimmte das Grundthema der Veranstaltung: die Kraft der Natur.

For the presentation of the 6th edition of the Hennessy Exclusive Collection the event concept was oriented on the image of the product. The cognac bottle, whose packaging takes the form of a boulder, determined the basic theme of the event: the power of nature.

Die Naturthematik war in erster Linie für die Auswahl des Ortes maßgebend. Als Location wurde deshalb die Schilfrohrflötenhöhle in der Nähe der chinesischen Stadt Guilin gewählt. Die tausend Jahre alte Kalksteinhöhle demonstrierte einerseits auf eindrucksvolle Weise die Kraft der Natur und bot andererseits ausreichend Platz für die Produktpräsentation und das Galadinner. Das natürliche Setting bestimmte aber auch die dramaturgische und dekorative Gestaltung des Events, denn die Bühnenshow setzte den Kalkstein und den See im Inneren der Höhle durch Licht- und Soundeffekte in den Mittelpunkt, Videos wurden direkt auf die Felswände projiziert und die Galatische waren in der Form von Felsbrocken gestaltet.

The nature theme was first and foremost important in selecting the venue. As such, the Reed Flute Cave near the Chinese city of Guilin was the chosen location. On the one hand the 1,000-year-old limestone cave impressively demonstrated the power of nature and on the other offered sufficient space for the product presentation and the gala dinner. Yet the natural setting also determined the dramaturgical and decorative design of the event, for the stage show focused attention on the limestone and the lake inside the cave by means of light and sound effects; videos were projected directly onto the cave walls and the gala tables were designed in the shape of boulders.

Die Intention der Veranstaltung lag also darin, durch die Inszenierung der natürlichen Kulisse die Hennessy Exclusive Collection VI dem Publikum als ein Produkt zu vermitteln, dessen Inhaltstoffe wie auch Aussehen von der Natur geformt wurden.

By setting the natural stage the event intended to communicate the Hennessy Exclusive Collection VI to the audience as a product whose ingredients as well as appearance are shaped by nature.

**Agency** Apax Group, Shanghai **Client** Moet Hennessy Diageo (China) Co. Ltd., Shanghai **Location** Reed Flute Cave, Guilin, China **Month/Year** December 2012 **Duration** Three days **Concept/Dramaturgy/Direction/Coordination/Architect/Graphics/Communications/Lighting/Films/Music/Artists/Showacts/Decoration/Construction** Apax Group **Media** Ruder Finn Asia **Catering** Sheraton **Photos** Apax Group

# Dine on the Line
# Siegelwerk

Location: Head quarter and manufacturing facility at the home of Rolls-Royce Motor Cars, Goodwood, UK

Wo sonst der Fertigungsprozess des neuen Phantom Series II abläuft, erlebten 130 von Rolls-Royce Motor Cars geladene Gäste eine Abendveranstaltung der besonderen Art – das Bankett-Dinner „Dine on the Line".

A group of 130 guests were invited by Rolls-Royce Motor Cars to gain an insight into the production process for the new Phantom Series II during a very special evening – namely, the banquet dinner "Dine on the Line".

Im Rahmen der Launch-Veranstaltung des neuen Phantom Series II lud der Hersteller seine Kunden in das Herz des Unternehmens, die Manufaktur in Großbritannien, ein. Speziell für diesen Anlass wurde die Produktionsstraße des Rolls-Royce-Werks innerhalb von fünf Tagen zu einer außergewöhnlichen Location umgebaut.

As part of the event's surrounding the launch of the new Phantom Series II, the automotive marque invited customers along to the company's nerve center in Great Britain. In a special operation just for the occasion, the company had the production line at the Rolls Royce works transformed into an extraordinary venue in just five days.

Nach der Ankunft auf dem Firmengelände betraten die Gäste über einen roten Teppich die hell erleuchtete gläserne Manufaktur. Dort erwartete sie am Ende der Produktionsstraße eine Cocktailbar mit Champagner, Kanapees und trockenen Martinis. Im Anschluss an die Begrüßungsrede durch den Vorstandsvorsitzenden Torsten Müller-Ötvös öffnete sich das Tor zum Dinner-bereich, wo die Gäste von zwei festlich gedeckten Tafeln sowie einem am Kopfende platzierten Phantom Series II erwartet wurden. Musikalisch durch den Abend begleitet wurden die Besucher vom Streich-quartett Escala. Nach Abschluss des Dinners öffnete sich die Bar-Lounge und bot ein entspanntes Ambiente zum Feiern und Kontakteknüpfen.

Der nächste Tag stand dann ganz im Zeichen des Fahr-erlebnisses und ermöglichte den Gästen, den neuen Phantom eingehend zu testen und zu erleben.

Upon arrival on the company grounds, the guests made their way down a red carpet into the brightly lit, glazed manufactory. There a cocktail bar was awaiting them at the end of the production line complete with cham-pagne, canapés and dry martinis. Following a welcome address from Chairman of the Management board Torsten Müller-Ötvös, the doors were opened to the dining area where guests were greeted by two festively laid tables and not forgetting a primly placed Phantom Series II at their head. And the evening was of course rounded out with a musical accompaniment in the form of the string quartet Escala. Once the plates had been cleared, the lounge bar was opened bringing the evening to a pleasant close in a relaxed atmosphere – a perfect combination of entertainment and networking.

The next day was dedicated to driver experience and guests were afforded the opportunity to test and experi-ence the new Phantom firsthand.

**Agency** Siegelwerk GmbH, Stuttgart **Client** Rolls-Royce Motor Cars, Westhampnett, Chichester, West Sussex, UK **Location** Head quarter and manufacturing facility at the home of Rolls-Royce Motor Cars, Goodwood, UK **Month / Year** May 2012 **Duration** Two days **Conception / Dramaturgy** Siegelwerk, Rolls-Royce Motor Cars **Direction / Coordination / Architecture / Graphics / Communication / Media / Decoration** Siegelwerk **Lighting** schoko pro GmbH **Music** Geschwister Schall **Artists / Showacts** Escala, Geschwister Schall **Catering** Cellar Society **Construction** Unit:Art GmbH **Photos** Barry Hayden, UK

# insglück

Location: Arena, Berlin, Germany

Im August 2012 lud Google über 700 Kreative aus Werbeagenturen zum „Summer of Creativity" in die Creative Sandbox zum Dialog über neue Möglichkeiten beim Online-Marketing und zur Entdeckungsreise durch die Google-Produktwelt ein.

In August 2012, Google invited over 700 creative professionals from advertising agencies to a Creative Sandbox: a dialog on new options for online marketing and a journey of discovery through the Google product world.

Veranstaltungslocation war die Arena in Berlin Kreuzberg. Deren Lage an der so genannten Berliner Media
Spree mit der dort angesiedelten Kreativindustrie und
der Sandstrand im Außenbereich unterstützten den
Sandbox-Gedanken.

Das Veranstaltungsdesign basierte auf dem Sandbox-
Logo, einem weißen, freien Raum, umrandet von den
Google-Farben. Ob im Plenum, in der Ausstellung oder
im Networking-Bereich, der weiße Raum wurde immer
wieder neu interpretiert.

In der Ausstellung wurden die Google-Produkte hap-
tisch umgesetzt, um die virtuellen Google-Tools und
-Kanäle in die reale Welt zu transportieren. Es entstand eine Mischung aus Think Tank, Spielwiese und
Erlebniswelt. Die Gäste konnten neueste Technologien
spielerisch erleben und sie mit der eigenen Kreativität
verknüpfen.

The venue for the "Summer of Creativity" was the Arena
in the Kreuzberg district of Berlin. Its location on the
so-called Berlin Media Spree with its creative industry
and sandy beach underscored the sandbox concept.

The recurring feature of the event was the sandbox logo,
a free white space edged by the Google colors. Whether
in the plenum, the exhibition or in the networking area,
the white space was repeatedly given a fresh interpretation.

In the exhibition the virtual Google tools and channels
were transported into the real world, and could actually
be tried out. The result was a mixture of think tank, play-
ground and hands-on experience. Guests could experience
the latest technology in a playful, experimental manner
and also bring in their own creativity.

ßenkunsttrend „Urban Knitting" – das Be- bzw. Umstri-
cken von Gegenständen – inspiriert und knüpfte an den
Start der Plattform als Do-it-yourself-Seite an. In der
Android Booth konnten jeweils zwei Besucher in einem
Tanzspiel gegeneinander antreten. Dabei wurden sie
als Android-Männchen auf einem Bildschirm gezeigt.

Drei von vier Kampagnen des mit einem Cannes Lion
ausgezeichneten „Re:Brief"-Projektes von Google
wurden im Wohnzimmerambiente der 1960er Jahre
vorgestellt. Es wurde gezeigt, wie erfolgreiche Werbe-
kampagnen der vergangenen 50 Jahre hätten aussehen können, wenn es die Google-Tools von heute
gegeben hätte.

The YouTube action box, for example, was inspired by
the street art trend "urban knitting" – involving knitting
around objects – and took up the start of the platform as
a do-it-yourself site. In the Android Booth two visitors
could dance against each other, and were depicted as
androids on a screen.

Three of the four campaigns from the Google "Re:Brief"
project, which received the Cannes Lion were presented
in a 1960s living room setting, demonstrating how successful advertising campaigns from the past fifty years
could have looked if today's Google tools had been available then.

**Agency** insglück Gesellschaft für Markeninszenierungen mbH, Berlin **Client** Google Germany GmbH, Hamburg **Location** Arena, Berlin, Germany **Month/Year** August 2012 **Duration** One day **Concept/Dramaturgy/Direction/Coordination/Graphics/Communication/Media/Music/Decoration** insglück **Stage architecture** Jan Pfeuffer **Lighting** Black Box Music Veranstaltungstechnik GmbH **Films** Mainpicture/Nonogos **Artists/Showacts** Julian Maier-Hauff, Osca Music, Reactable Anton Furner, DJ Twizzstar **Catering** Einhorn Catering **Construction** Balloni GmbH **Photos** Markus Mielek

# Audi A6L Launch 2012
## China Kingway Communications, Planwerkstatt

Location: International Sports Arena, Guangzhou, China

Im März 2012 lud Audi zum Launch seines neuesten Modells A6L. Schauplatz des Events war die International Sports Arena in Guangzhou, deren Inneres für diesen Anlass durch den Einbau einer 200 t schweren Stahlkonstruktion in eine vierstöckige Fahrbahn umgestaltet wurde.

In March 2012, Audi invited guests to the launch of its latest model, A6L. The venue: the International Sports Arena in Guangzhou, whose interior was transformed into a four-storey track for the event by installing a steel structure weighing 200 t.

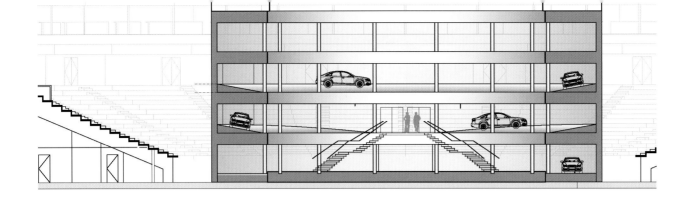

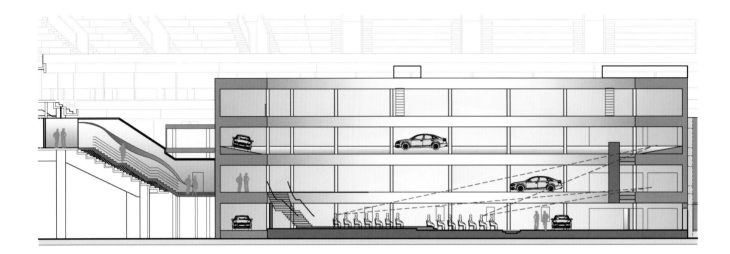

Auch die Fassade des Stadions wurde entsprechend verändert und um einen Empfangsbereich erweitert, der sich harmonisch in die bestehende Glas- und Aluminiumkonstruktion einfügte. Dort erwartete die Besucher ein futuristisches Ambiente mit netzartigem Dekor und einer interaktiven Erlebniswelt.

Im Innern des Stadions wurde ein komplexes Arrangement aus vier kreisförmigen Ebenen errichtet, welche im Zentrum eine theaterähnliche Bühne mitsamt Zuschauerbereich umschlossen. Auf diesen übereinander angeordneten Spuren, die ähnlich wie eine Reihe von Galerien angelegt waren, fuhren die neuen Audi-Modelle ihre Bahnen und präsentierten sich so den Zuschauern als aktiver Teil der Inszenierung.

The arena's façade was also altered, and a reception area was added, which fitted harmoniously into the existing glass and aluminum construction. A futuristic setting with net-like décor and interactive experiences awaited visitors there.

Inside the arena a complex arrangement of four circular runways was erected enclosing a theater stage with an area for spectators at its center. The new Audi models drove on these runways, which were arranged above each other like a series of galleries, enabling spectators to experience them as an active part of the event.

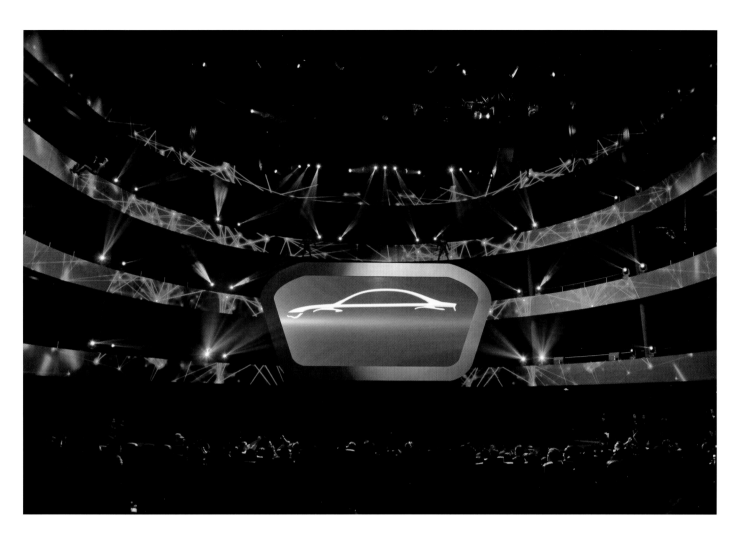

Die Gestalt der zentralen LED-Wand griff die Form des Kühlergrills des neuen A6L-Modells auf. Auch die befahrbare Hauptbühne war im Design an die Formensprache Audis angelehnt und bot Raum für Präsentationen, musikalische Darbietungen und Showeinlagen der Luftakrobaten. Die drei Themenwelten Audis – ultra, e-tron und connect – wurden dabei innerhalb des kulturellen Rahmenprogramms entsprechend in Szene gesetzt.

Anschließend wechselten die Gäste über die Bühne in einen anderen Raum, wo ein ganzes Arsenal schwebender Leuchtkörper warmes Licht verbreitete. Das Zentrum des Raums bildete eine von einer LED-Wand flankierte Entertainmentbühne. Hier fand das Event mit einem festlichen Dinner seinen Abschluss.

The design of the central LED screen reflected the shape of the radiator grill of the new A6L. Similarly, the styling of the main stage was inspired by the Audi design language and provided space for presentations, musical performances and the skills of the trapeze artists. Audi's three topical worlds – ultra, e-tron and connect – were staged within the accompanying cultural program.

Subsequently, guests moved via the stage to another area, where a whole arsenal of suspended luminaires gave off a warm light. At the center of the room stood an entertainment stage flanked by an LED screen, where a festive evening meal concluded the event.

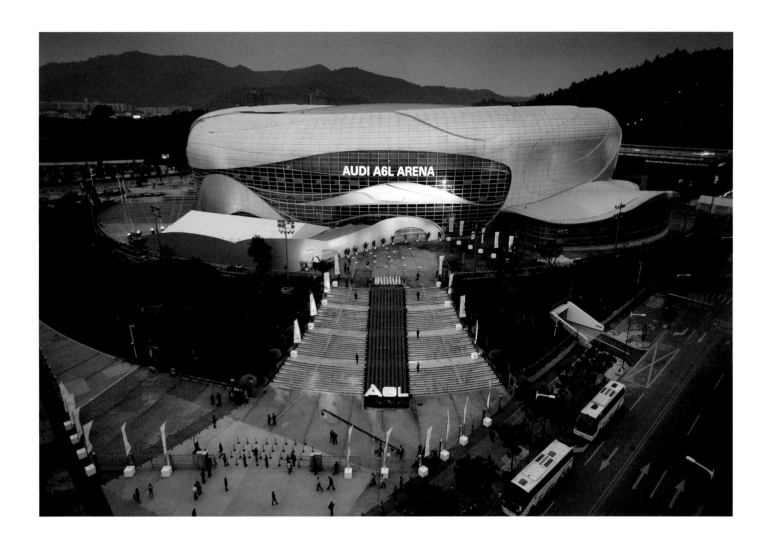

**Agency** China Kingway Communications, Beijing **Client** FAW Volkswagen Automotive Co. Ltd, Changchun **Location** International Sports Arena, Guangzhou, China **Month/Year** March 2012 **Duration** Several days **Concept/Dramaturgy/Direction/Coordination** China Kingway Communications **Architecture/Decoration** Planwerkstatt GmbH, Bedburg-Hau **Graphics/Communication** Planwerkstatt (concept), China Kingway Communications (realisation) **Media** China Kingway Communications, Creators GmbH **Lighting** Kingsmark Event Engineering Co. Ltd, Shanghai **Artists/Showacts** Dancing Bears **Car choreography** Quintons Concept **Construction** Pico Messebau, Beijing **Photos** China Kingway Communications

# Inauguration Ceremony of Minera Esperanza
## MAA Architecture - Design - Communication

Location: Truck Shop Minera Esperanza, Calama, Sierra Gorda, Region of Antofagasta, Chile

Um die Einweihung eines neuen Bergbaubetriebs zu feiern, lud der chilenische Bergbaukonzern Antofagasta Minerals im April 2012 seine Kunden, Mitarbeiter und zahlreiche weitere Gäste, darunter auch der chilenische Staatspräsident, zu einer Galaveranstaltung ein.

To celebrate the inauguration of a new mine in April 2012 Chilenian mining corporation Antofagasta Minerals invited its customers, employees and numerous other guests, including the President of Chile, to a gala event.

Das neueröffnete Bergwerk Minera Esperanza soll in den ersten zehn Jahren seines Betriebs 190.000 t Kupfer und als Nebenprodukt 230.000 Pfund Gold abbauen. Dabei kommt weltweit erstmals eine innovative Technik zur Anwendung, bei der unbehandeltes Meerwasser über eine 175 km lange Pipeline herbeigeleitet und zur Gewinnung von Kupferkonzentrat verwendet wird.

Grundidee des Abends war es, die Gäste mit den unterschiedlichen Verfahren, Arbeitsabläufen und Zusammenhängen des Bergbauprojekts vertraut zu machen. Auch die Ausmaße des Projektes in Hinsicht auf schiere Größe, Aufwand, Betriebskapital und Infrastruktur sollten entsprechend wiedergegeben werden.

In the first ten years of operation the newly-opened mine Minera Esperanza is to produce 190,000 t of copper and, as a by-product, 230,000 pounds of gold. An innovative technique will be employed for the first time in the world: untreated seawater introduced via a 175 km long pipeline will serve to mine the copper concentrate.

The basic idea behind the evening was to familiarize guests with the various techniques, processes and circumstances related to the mining project. Another aim was to demonstrate the scale of the project as regards sheer size, operating capital and infrastructure.

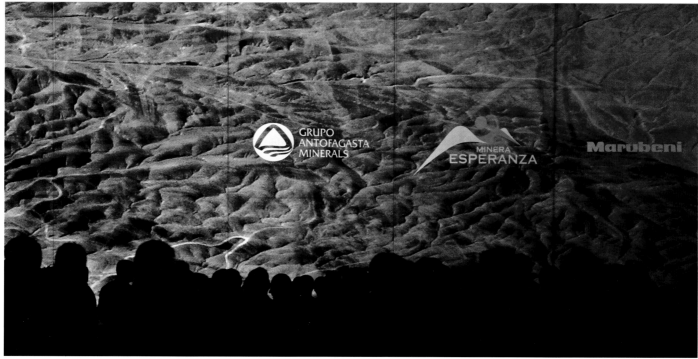

Die Vermittlung all dieser Inhalte erfolgte größtenteils über vier große Präsentationsflächen aus hochdichtem Styropor, auf denen die wichtigsten Aspekte der Kupfergewinnung zusammengefasst und projiziert wurden. Das hier gezeigte audiovisuelle Material bot zudem reichhaltige Hintergrundinformationen zur Minera Esperanza. Begleitet wurde die Präsentation von einer eigens zu diesem Anlass komponierten Musik, die vom lokalen Philharmonieorchester aufgeführt wurde.

Durch eine Kombination von räumlichen, audiovisuellen und grafischen Elementen gelang es, schwer vermittelbare technische und wirtschaftliche Inhalte in eine beeindruckende Präsentation und Erfahrung umzusetzen.

For the most part this information was conveyed via four large presentation surfaces of high-density polystyrene, on which the key aspects of copper extraction were summarized and projected. This audio-visual material also provided extensive background information about Minera Esperanza. The presentation was accompanied by music especially composed for the occasion and performed by the local orchestra.

This combination of three-dimensional, audio-visual and graphic elements succeeded in presenting complicated technical and economic information comprehensibly in an impressive show.

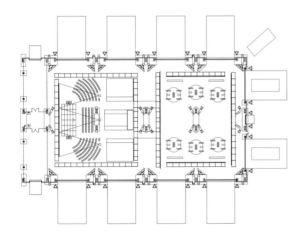

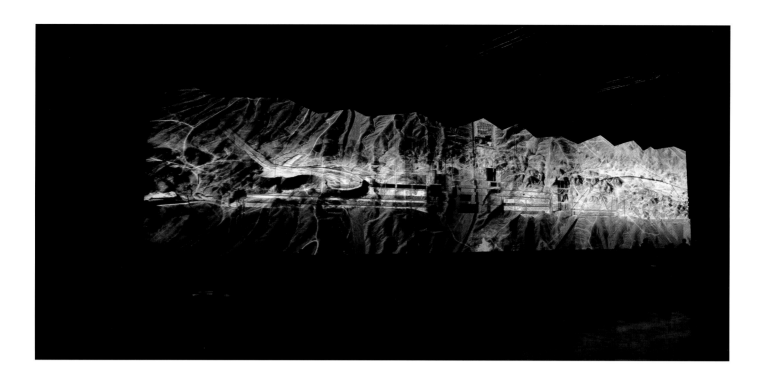

**Agency** MAA Architecture – Design – Communication, Santiago de Chile **Client** Antofagasta Minerals / Minera Esperanza, Santiago **Location** Truck Shop Minera Esperanza, Calama, Sierra Gorda, Region of Antofagasta, Chile **Month / Year** April 2012 **Duration** One day **Conception / Dramaturgy / Direction / Coordination / Lighting / Films / Decoration / Construction** MAA Architecture – Design – Communication **Architecture** Agustín Quiroga, Pedro Casto **Graphics / Communication** Nicolás Galdames **Media** Proyecto Led **Music / Artists / Showacts** Simón Poblete **Catering** CPC Eventos **Photos** Daniel Motecinos, Santiago

# Audi Q3 Launch
## marbet, CREATORS, Planwerkstatt

Location: Gymnasium Guangzhou, China

Im Juli 2012 feierte Audi die China-Einführung des neuen Q3. Pressevertreter, Händler und Kunden waren eingeladen, sich von den Vorzügen des Kompakt-SUVs zu überzeugen.

In July 2012, Audi celebrated the launch of the new Q3 in China. Press representatives, dealers and customers were invited to be convinced of the benefits of the compact SUV.

findenden Audi Cups – mit dem Spiel FC Bayern München gegen VfL Wolfsburg –, präsentierte sich die Markteinführung des Q3 als unterhaltsamer Party-abend. Unter dem Motto „Thrill your City" erlebten die Besucher eine Mischung aus modernem Lifestyle und mitreißenden Fußballmomenten.

Architektonisch wurde eine urbane, inspirierende At-mosphäre geschaffen. Die Veranstaltung war in drei Ebenen unterteilt, die sich aufeinander aufbauend zu einem großen Erlebnisraum verdichteten: die Fußball-arena, das Q3-Launch-Theater sowie die Fußball- und Lifestyle-World.

Besonderes Merkmal des Events war die enge Verzah-nung von Architektur, Kommunikation und medialer Bespielung. Ein zentrales Element der Inszenierung waren die interaktiven LED-Cubes, die – wie alle medial bespielbaren Flächen – live auf die Fahrbewegungen der vorgestellten Q3-Modelle reagierten.

Coinciding with the opening of the Audi Cup the follow-ing day – with the soccer match between FC Bayern Munich and VfL Wolfsburg – the launch of the Q3 was presented as an entertaining party evening. Under the motto "Thrill your City" visitors experienced a mix of modern lifestyle and exciting soccer moments.

Architecturally, an urban, inspiring atmosphere was created. The event was divided into three levels, which when combined with one another produced a wealth of experiences: the soccer arena, the Q3 Launch Theater and the Soccer and Lifestyle World.

What really set the event apart was the close dovetailing of architecture, communication and medial performance. A key element of the presentation were the interactive LED cubes, which – like all the surfaces on which media could be presented – responded "live" to the movement of the showcased Q3 models.

Im Rahmen der anschließenden After-Show-Party wurde der Unterhaltungs- und Interaktionsgedanke des Events fortgeführt. Verschiedene Installationen und Themenbereiche wie etwa Car Painting, interaktive Informationsterminals und Football Lounges gaben den Gästen Gelegenheit, die Welt des Q3 und des Audi Cup China weiter zu erforschen.

The entertainment and interaction concept was continued in the framework of the after show party. Various installations and topical areas such as car painting, interactive information terminals and soccer lounges, gave guests the opportunity to explore the world of the Q3 and the Audi Cup China.

**Agency** marbet Marion & Bettina Würth GmbH & Co. KG, Künzelsau; CREATORS GmbH, Darmstadt; Planwerkstatt, Bedburg-Hau **Client** FAW-VW Audi Sales Division China, Changchun **Location** Gymnasium Guangzhou, China **Month/Year** July 2012 **Duration** One evening **Concept/Dramaturgy** marbet, CREATORS **Direction/Coordination** marbet, CREATORS, Planwerkstatt **Architecture** Planwerkstatt, Kim & Fischer Architekten **Graphics/Communication** Jane Fox Werbeagentur **Media** CREATORS **Lighting** Modern Times **Artists/Showacts** marbet Deutschland **Decoration** D&T China **Catering** Shangri-La **Construction** Planwerkstatt, D&T China **Photos** Jens Thoben

# Bilstein's 100ᵗʰ Anniversary
## Uniplan, Late Night Concepts

Location: Hagen-Hohenlimburg, Germany

Das zweitägige Event – bestehend aus Abendgala für Lieferanten und Kunden sowie einem Mitarbeitertag – wurde anlässlich des hundertjährigen Bestehens der Bilstein Kaltband Walzwerke direkt am Firmensitz in Hagen-Hohenlimburg veranstaltet.

This two-day event comprising an evening gala for suppliers and customers and a day for employees was held at the company headquarters itself in Hagen-Hohenlimburg to celebrate the 100th anniversary of Bilstein Kaltband Walzwerke.

Weg des Stahls – von der Entstehung über den Walz-
prozess bis hin zum Endprodukt. Die Inszenierung fand
in einem 8-Master-Zelt statt, in das ein Empfangs- und
Veranstaltungsbereich integriert wurden. Die Gäste
der Gala wurden Teil einer 360°-Rauminszenierung
mit interaktiven, auf die Architektur projizierten Vi-
deosequenzen, Live-Musikern, Akrobaten, kinetischen
Effekten und Pyrotechnik. Geschwindigkeit, Hitze und
Präzision der Stahlerzeugung wurden körperlich er-
fahrbar. Höhepunkt der Show war eine „Stahlsinfonie",
live gespielt von Musikern in einem abstrahierten
Hochregallager auf Produkten aus Stahl.

The dramaturgy of the evening reflected the development of steel from its formation via the rolling process
through to the final product. The presentation took place
in an eight-mast marquee incorporating a reception and
event area. Guests to the gala became part of a 360°
show featuring interactive video sequences projected
onto the architecture, live musicians, acrobats, kinetic
effects and pyrotechnics. Guests experienced first-hand
the speed, heat and precision involved in steel production. The highlight of the show: a "steel symphony",
music performed live on steel products in an abstract
high-bay warehouse.

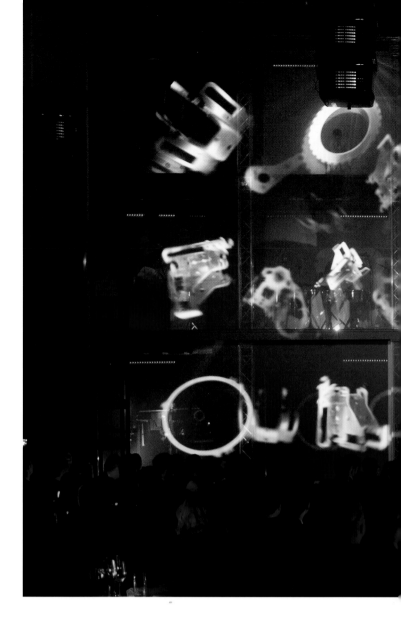

Unter dem Motto „Faszination Stahl" stand auch das Jubiläumsfest für die Mitarbeiter. In sechs Länderpavillons wurden den über 3.000 Gästen die Auslandsstandorte der Bilstein-Gruppe mit landestypischer Musik, Showacts und zahlreichen Mitmach-Aktionen präsentiert.

The fascination of steel was also the motto of the anniversary celebration for employees. In six national pavilions the locations of the Bilstein Group outside Germany were presented to over 3,000 guests with typical national music, show acts and numerous events for guests to join in.

**Agency** Uniplan GmbH & Co. KG, Cologne **Client** Bilstein Gruppe, Hagen-Hohenlimburg **Location** Hagen-Hohenlimburg, Germany **Month/Year** July 2011 **Duration** Two days **Concept/Dramaturgy** Uniplan, Tobias Stupeler **Direction/Coordination** Rüdiger Kloep **Architecture** Lennart Günther **Graphics/Communication** Uniplan **Media/Films/Music** Phase 7 **Lighting** Björn Hermann **Showacts/Artists** 15/08 Entertainment, Phase 7 **Scenics/Decoration** Late Night Concepts GmbH & Co. KG, Werne; Ingo Kaiser **Catering** Kirberg Catering **Construction** Rüdiger Kloep **Photos** Leonard Billeke

# Trend Event 2017 –
# Michelin Summer Roadtrip
## Emmy B.

Location: maxwood Hochseilgarten, Lüneburg; Schloss Weissenstein, Pommersfelden, Germany

Auch im Sommer 2012 veranstalteten die Michelin Reifenwerke aus Karlsruhe wieder ihr mittlerweile traditionelles Friend Event. Mehr als 720 Kunden aus Reifen- und Autohandel nahmen diesmal an einer zweiwöchigen Sommer-Rallye teil.

In summer 2012, Karlsruhe-based tire manufacturer Michelin Reifenwerke once again held its Friend Event, now something of a tradition. This year's event welcomed more than 720 customers from tire and automotive retail to take part in a two-week summer rally.

Ziel der Rallye war es, die Reifen-Neueinführungen des Jahres 2012 im Bereich PKW zu präsentieren und dabei gleichzeitig die Kundenbindung und die Präsenz der Marke Michelin im Bewusstsein der Händler zu stärken.

Die Cabrio-Rallye erstreckte sich über sechs verschiedene Stationen. Im Fahrsicherheitszentrum wurden an den ersten beiden Stationen die neuen Produkte von Michelin getestet. Anschließend wurden die Reifenhändler beim Lösen eines überdimensionalen Kreuzworträtsels an das Thema EU-Labeling herangeführt. Ein Segway-Parcours und ein Vortrag über Körpersprache rundeten das Angebot ab. Zum Abschluss wurden die neuen Produkte für Sommer und Winter vorgestellt.

The aim of the rally was to present the tire manufacturer's new product launches for 2012 in the passenger car segment and simultaneously strengthen the Michelin brand's connection to its customers and root its presence in the awareness of retailers.

The convertible rally took place across six different stations. The new Michelin products were tested at the first two stations at driving safety centers. Then, while solving a giant crossword puzzle, the tire retailers were able to familiarize themselves with the topic of EU labeling. This was followed by a Segway tour and a talk on body language. Then to round out the program, the new summer and winter products were presented to the group.

Die Abendveranstaltung fand im Michelin Glamping Camp statt, das speziell für diese Gelegenheit angelegt wurde. Die vierzig komfortabel ausgestatteten Safarizelte boten eine ebenso bequeme wie ungewöhnliche Übernachtungslocation. Der Höhepunkt der Veranstaltung wurde auf einer 350 m² großen Terrasse unter den Dächern von nordischen Katanzelten in Szene gesetzt: Beim Barbecue mit Lagerfeuerstimmung konnte man den Abend ausklingen lassen.

An evening event was then held at the Michelin glamping camp, which had been installed especially for the occasion. The accommodation – 40 comfortably furnished safari tents – made for a cozy and unique overnight experience. The highlight of the event was unveiled on a 350-m² terrace under the cover of traditional Nordic tents, where the group saw out the evening with a barbecue and a cozy campfire atmosphere.

**Agency** Emmy B. GmbH live communication, Stuttgart **Client** Michelin Reifenwerke AG & Co. KGaA, Karlsruhe **Location** maxwood Hochseilgarten Lüneburg; Schloss Weissenstein, Pommersfelden, Germany **Month / Year** June 2012 **Duration** Two weeks **Concept / Dramaturgy / Direction / Coordination / Architecture** Emmy B. **Catering** Stefan Marquardt Event Catering, Tutzing **Construction** Freibauten GmbH, Stuttgart; Luxe Tenten B. V., Emmeloord **Photos** Thorben Jäger, Stuttgart

# Industrial Theater

Location: City hall Karlsruhe, Germany

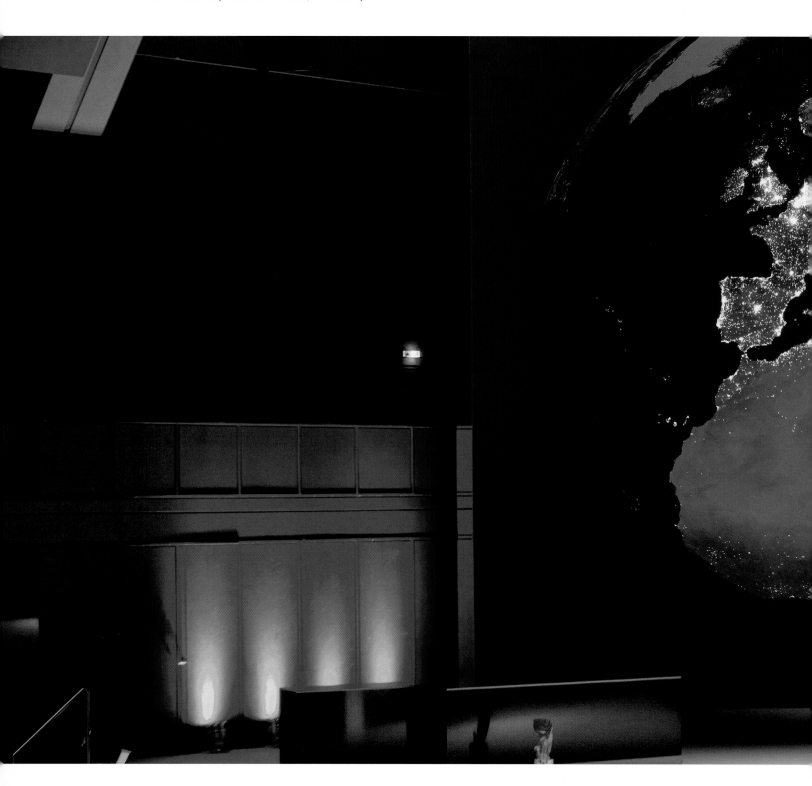

TH New Yea Receptio 20 3

Das 200-jährige Bestehen der Industrie- und Handels-kammer (IHK) Karlsruhe war Anlass für eine feierliche Veranstaltung im Rahmen des alljährlichen Neujahrs-empfangs. 1.600 Gäste aus Industrie, Handel, Politik und Öffentlichkeit nahmen an dem einmaligen Ereignis teil.

To celebrate the 200th anniversary of the Karlsruhe Chamber of Commerce and Industry (IHK) a special event was held as part of its annual New Year reception. 1,600 guests from the worlds of industry, commerce, politics and public life attended the one-off event.

Um die Jubiläumsveranstaltung zu einem dramaturgischen Highlight zu machen, wurden die Reden und Grußworte von einer anschaulichen Präsentation der Geschichte der IHK, ihres Handlungsfeldes und ihres zukunftsweisenden Engagements begleitet.

Das Zentrum der Bühne bildete ein Objekt von 10x10m Größe, das eine Rundprojektionsfläche von 8m Durchmesser freigab und das Schlussbild einer sich im Raum frei drehenden Weltkugel entstehen ließ. In drei Kurzfilmen wurde die komplette Geschichte der IHK Karlsruhe – von ihrem Gründungsakt 1813 bis hin zur Etablierung als Interessenvertretung von aktuell 67.000 Mitgliedern – und die weltweit vernetzte Technologieregion Karlsruhe präsentiert.

Durch die virtuose Abstimmung von Projektionsinhalten und Musik – teils live, teils eingespielt – wurde die Inszenierung zum tatsächlichen Kunstwerk. Höhepunkt bildete die Uraufführung des sechzehnhändigen Klavierstücks „Zeit", das von acht Pianisten an vier Flügeln vorgetragen und von Urmas Sisask für diesen Anlass komponiert worden war. Das Konzept überzeugte durch seine klare Dramaturgie und wurde auch vonseiten der Presse positiv angenommen.

To make the anniversary event a theatrical highlight, the speeches and words of welcome were accompanied by a lively presentation of the history of the IHK, its scope of action and its pioneering commitment.

At the center of the stage was an object measuring 10x10m, which revealed a round projection screen with an 8m diameter, thus creating a final impression of a globe spinning freely in the space. Three short films showed the entire history of the IHK Karlsruhe from its foundation through to its establishment as a body representing the interests of its (currently) 67,000 members, as well as showcasing the Karlsruhe region as a globally-networked center of technology.

Thanks to the excellent coordination of projections and the partly recorded and partly live music, the presentation was a true work of art. It culminated in the premiere of the 16-handed piano piece "Zeit" (Time), which was performed by eight pianists on four concert pianos and which Urmas Sisask had composed especially for the occasion. The concept was a resounding success owing to the clear theatrical format, and also received positive press coverage.

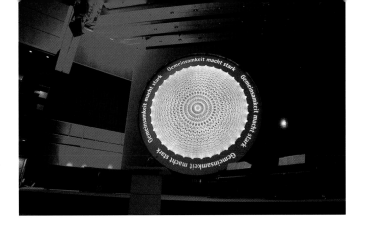

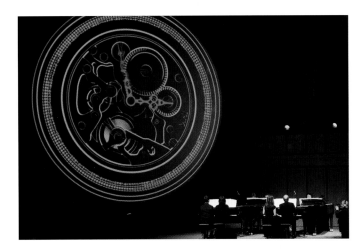

Auf diese Weise präsentierte die Jubiläumsfeier die IHK Karlsruhe nicht in historisierenden Bildern, sondern mit modernen Mitteln in Design, Dramaturgie, Bühnenbau und komplex gebauten Projektionsinhalten. Die Veranstaltung vermittelte eine klare Botschaft: Es geht um gelebtes Gegenwartsdenken mit zukunftsgerichtetem Blick auf Tradition basierende Moderne – bodenständig und visionär.

All in all, the celebration did not present the IHK Karlsruhe in historicizing images, but relied on modern means in design, dramaturgy and staging, teamed with complex projections. The event communicated a clear message: the IHK Karlsruhe is firmly anchored in the present, with its sights set on the future, modern but with a strong tradition, down-to-earth yet visionary.

**Agency** Industrial Theater, Karlsruhe **Client** Industrie- und Handelskammer Karlsruhe **Location** City hall Karlsruhe, Germany **Month / Year** Januar 2013 **Duration** One day **Concept / Dramaturgy** Enno-Ilka Uhde, Industrial Theater **Direction / Coordination** Enno-Ilka Uhde **Communication** IHK Karlsruhe **Lighting** KMK GmbH, Stage Concept GmbH **Films** Industrial Theater, Enno-Ilka Uhde, Maria Spahn **Artists / Music** Sontraud Speidel, Saule Tatubaeva, Kalle Randalu, Toomas Vana and students of the University of Music Karlsruhe; Urmas Sisask **Decoration** Industrial Theater, WE make it GmbH **Construction** Stage Concept, WE make it **Photos** Daniel Weckert (Industrial Theater), Thuy Nguyen (in nihilo)

# Mercedes-Benz International Dealer Conference Davos 2012
## Agentur für Marken(t)räume

Location: Davos Congress Center, Davos Eishalle, Switzerland

Davos, die höchstgelegene Stadt Europas, wurde im Mai 2012 für die Dauer der Händlertagung des Unternehmens Mercedes-Benz zum Basislager für 2.500 Markenrepräsentanten aus ganz Europa.

Davos, the highest town in Europe, was transformed in May 2012 for the duration of the Mercedes-Benz dealer conference into a base camp for 2,500 representatives of the marque from all over Europe.

Das Basislager bestand aus drei Hotspots: der Eishalle, dem Congress Center und dem Big-Biwak-Zelt – ergänzt durch das „Höhencamp" Schatzalp und eine Outdoor-Area mit Parcours. Inszenierung, Set Design und Szenografie sowie Performances und Medien wurden unter dem Motto „To the top." auf die Eventziele und die Anmutung der Locations abgestimmt. Die Eishalle wurde so zum Ort der „Keynote Statements" und der Markeninszenierung, das Congress Center zum Schauplatz für Plenum-Sessions, den Infomarkt, Länder-Meetings und die Abschlussinszenierung, die Schatzalp zum Vorstellungsort der neuen A-Klasse und des Citans.

The base camp consisted of three hot spots: the Ice Hockey Arena, the Congress Center and the Large Bivouac Tent – rounded out by the "Heights Camp" on the Schatzalp and an Outdoor Area with a course to surmount. The staging, set design, and scenography as well as the performances and media were all designed with the slogan "To the top." in mind and customized to the goals of the events and the feel of the locations. The Ice Hockey Arena thusmorphed into the venue for the "keynote statements" and for staging the marque, the Congress Center was the location for the plenary sessions, the information market, the country meetings and the final set, while the Schatzalp was used to present the new A-class and the Citan.

Ein multifunktionales Online-Tool gewährleistete die reibungslose Abwicklung des Teilnehmermanagements. Eine umfangreiche App mit Präsentationen, fahrzeugspezifischen Details sowie weiterführendem Text- und Bildmaterial war die Basis für mehrere Workshops.

Verschiedenartige Interaktionsangebote, Workshops und Medien sowie eine spektakuläre Markeninszenierung vermittelten sinnbildlich die notwendigen Qualitäten für eine Bergbesteigung. „To the top." wurde dramaturgisch, architektonisch, medial und inszenatorisch als ausgefeiltes Gesamterlebnis gestaltet und hat die Teilnehmer so auf den gemeinsamen „Gipfelsturm" vorbereitet.

A multifunctional online tool ensured smooth management of the conference participants. An extensive App including presentations, vehicle-specific details and in-depth texts and image materials formed the basis for several workshops.

Different types of interactive services, workshops and media as well as a spectacular staging of the marque all combined to symbolize the qualities you need to climb a mountain - to all the senses. "To the top." was transformed dramatically, architecturally, and in terms of media and set design into an ingenious all-round experience and thus prepared participants for the final "assault on the peak" together.

**Agency** Agentur für Marken(t)räume GmbH, Esslingen **Client** Daimler AG, Stuttgart **Location** Davos Congress Center, Davos Eishalle, Big Biwak, Switzerland **Month / Year** May 2012 **Duration** Four days **Conception / Dramaturgy** Agentur für Marken(t)räume, zet:project. GmbH **Direction / Coordination / Architecture / Graphics / Communication** Agentur für Marken(t)räume **Media / Films** zet:project. **Lighting** music & light design GmbH, rgb GmbH **Music / Artists / Showacts** Mönchspfeffer GmbH **Construction** metron GmbH **Photos** Andreas Keller, Altdorf; Uli Jooss, Aichtal **Awards** EVA Award (bronze), Adam & EVA audience award, iF communication design award 2013

# EMPLOYEE EVENT

# EuroTraining 2012
## "Inspired for a new generation"
## STAGG & FRIENDS

Location: Event Island, Berlin, Germany

Mit einer außergewöhnlichen Trainings- und Qualifizie-
rungsmaßnahme bereitete die Daimler AG im Sommer
2012 ihre Vertriebsmannschaft auf die neuen Themen
und Produkte des Konzerns vor.

In summer 2012, Daimler AG conducted an unusual
training and qualification event to familiarize its sales
team with the company's new topics and products.

Insgesamt 15.000 Teilnehmer aus 51 Ländern wurden im Laufe von drei Monaten in die Details der neuen A-Klasse und etlicher weiterer Neuheiten – unter anderem des neuen CLS Shooting Brake – eingewiesen.

Die Inszenierung des EuroTrainings war dramaturgisch wie ein Citytrip angelegt. Hierfür wurde die Industrielandschaft der Insel Eiswerder in mehrere Bereiche unterteilt, die den verschiedenen Produkten und Themen zugeordnet waren. Der Schwerpunkt lag dabei auf der neuen A-Klasse, deren Location einem Berliner Szeneviertel nachempfunden war.

In the course of three months some 15,000 employees from 51 nations were briefed on the details of the new A-class and a host of other new products including the new CLS Shooting Brake.

The EuroTraining program was structured in the manner of a city trip. Specifically, the industrial landscape of the island Eiswerder was divided into several sections, which were assigned to the various products and topics. The focus was on the new A-class, whose location was modeled on a hip Berlin district.

Die Trainingsstationen waren als authentisches Lebensumfeld der Zielgruppe gestaltet. Dadurch entstand eine Produkt- und Markenlandschaft, die nicht nur die Formensprache von Mercedes-Benz aufgriff, sondern diese auch modern und neu interpretierte. Über interaktive Präsentationsmodule wie Touchscreens und iPads – in Kombination mit analogen Methoden – wurden die Lerninhalte vermittelt und bildeten einen direkten Bezug zu den Kaufmotiven der Kunden.

Das Kommunikationskonzept der Veranstaltung lehnte sich stark an die aktuelle Kampagne für die A-Klasse an. Acht Kuben erinnerten an eine urbane Umgebung – daneben gab es einen Coffee Shop, einen Music Store, einen Digital-Lifestyle- und Add-on-Store sowie ein großes Loft. In diese waren intuitiv bedienbare Trainingsstationen integriert, die zu einem spielerischen Umgang mit den Trainingsinhalten einluden.

The training stations were designed as authentic settings of the target group, creating a product and brand landscape, which not only reflected the design language of Mercedes-Benz but also gave it a fresh, modern interpretation. The instruction content was communicated via interactive presentation modules such as touchscreens and iPads in conjunction with analog methods, and had a direct link to the customers' buying motives.

The communication concept for the event was modeled heavily on the current campaign for the A-class. With eight cubes evoking an urban setting, there was also a coffee shop, a music store, as well as a digital lifestyle and add-on store. Finally, there was a large loft equipped with intuitive training terminals inviting participants to engage with the training content in a playful fashion.

Interaktive Elemente und Medienbespielungen sowie die Vernetzung mit Social-Media-Elementen und Guerilla-Aktionen im Zentrum Berlins machten deutlich, dass Mercedes-Benz hier eine neue Generation von Trainingsveranstaltungen vorgestellt hatte.

Interactive elements and media projections, not to mention networking with social media elements and guerilla actions in the center of Berlin demonstrated that Mercedes-Benz was presenting a new generation of training events.

**Agency** STAGG & FRIENDS GmbH, Düsseldorf **Client** Daimler AG, Stuttgart **Location** event island, Berlin, Germany **Month / Year** June-August 2012 **Duration** Three months **Conception / Dramaturgy / Direction / Coordination / Decoration** STAGG & FRIENDS **Architecture / Graphics / Communication** dan pearlman GmbH **Media / Films** Andreas Roos **Lighting** Sound & Light Veranstaltungstechnik GmbH **Construction** Artlife GmbH **Photos** diephotodesigner.de OHG, Berlin **Awards** EVA-Award

# Roche Diabetes Care Germany Annual Conference 2012 "Ready to Emerge"

## insglück

Location: Berlin, Germany

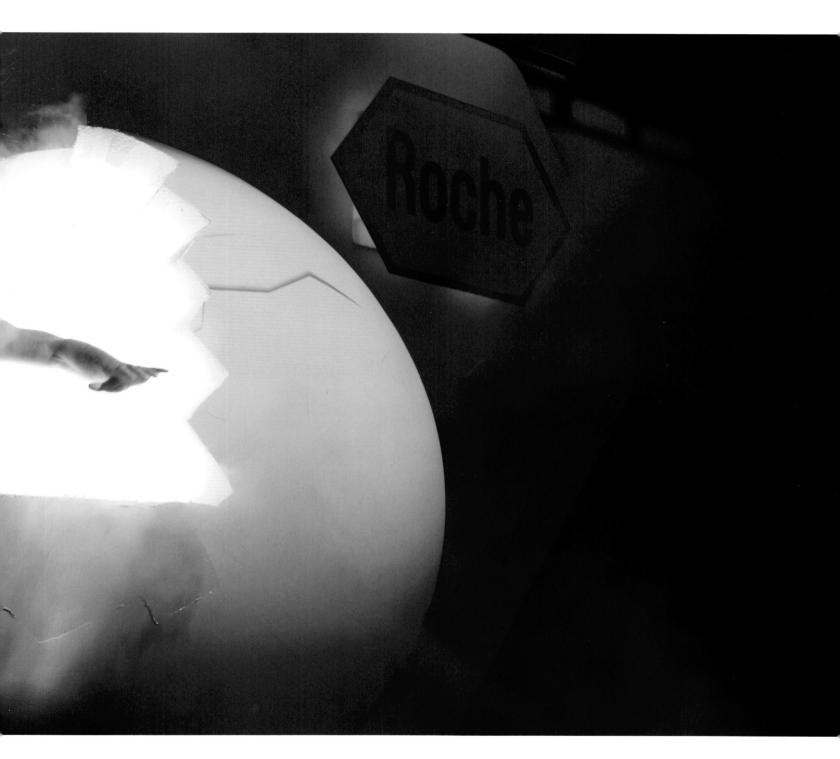

Für die Diabetes-Sparte der Roche Diagnostics Deutschland GmbH war die Jahrestagung in Berlin gleichzeitig der Startschuss für die Einführung einer neuen Organisationsstruktur.

For the Diabetes unit of Roche Diagnostics Deutschland GmbH, the annual conference in Berlin also marked the launch of a new organizational structure.

Roche Diabetes Care Deutschland, der Diabetes-Anbieter von Roche Diagnostics, hat einen intensiven Veränderungsprozess durchlaufen: neue Geschäftsfelder wurden geschaffen, Kompetenzen neu verteilt und Prozesse neu definiert. All diese Neuerungen fordern von den Mitarbeitern eine große Veränderungsbereitschaft und ein hohes Engagement. Die Jahrestagung in Berlin sollte für mehr als 300 Vertriebsmitarbeiter zugleich Kick-off und Motivation für die neue Organisationsstruktur sein.

Zentrales Element der Veranstaltung war ein überdimensionales, im Raum stehendes Ei – als Sinnbild für neues Leben, Potential und Neubeginn. Zwei Tage lang stand das Ei im Mittelpunkt verschiedener interaktiver Module, wobei es durch den Input der Teilnehmer immer weiter verändert wurde, bis es als Metapher für den Neustart schließlich aufbrach.

Roche Diabetes Care Deutschland, the Diabetes unit of Roche Diagnostics, has undergone an intensive process of changes: new business fields were created, responsibilities reassigned and processes redefined. All these innovations demand from employees a great willingness to embrace change and a high level of commitment. For more than 300 sales staff, the annual conference in Berlin was also intended to mark the launch of the new organizational structure and motivate employees.

The focal element of the event was a larger-than-life egg – symbolic of new life, potential and new beginnings. For two days the egg stood at the center of various interactive modules, and thanks to input by the participants it was increasingly altered until it burst open as a metaphor for the new start.

Der erste Tagungstag bereitete den Aufbruch vor. Hintergründe und Notwendigkeit der Veränderungen wurden transparent gemacht. Management und Mitarbeiter tauschten sich im direkten Dialog aus. Eine Vielzahl von Formaten rund um das Ei sorgte für Verständnis, Aktivierung und ein Gefühl für Gemeinschaft. Der zum Abschluss inszenierte erste Riss im Ei bildete den vielversprechenden Ausklang des ersten Tages.

Im Mittelpunkt des zweiten Tages stand eine Mitarbeiteraktion: In 33 Workshop-Gruppen entwickelten diese den neuen internen Claim des Unternehmens. Der Sieger-Claim wurde in einem spannenden Voting wie beim Eurovision Song Contest ermittelt. Das anschließend aufbrechende Ei machte dann den Neubeginn sichtbar – Aufbruchsstimmung in jedem Sinne.

The first day of the conference paved the way for the new start. Reasons for the existing situation were outlined, and the need for change was explained. Management and employees engaged in direct exchange with one another. A large number of formats relating to the egg generated understanding, activation and a sense of community. The first crack that was produced at the end made for a promising conclusion to the first day.

The focus of the second day was on an employee action: split into 33 workshop groups, employees looked to create a new internal corporate claim. The winning claim was chosen by a voting system based on the Eurovision Song Contest. The new beginning was visualized by the egg subsequently bursting open completely: a cracking new start in every sense of the word.

**Agency** insglück Gesellschaft für Markeninszenierungen mbH, Berlin **Client** Roche Diagnostics Deutschland GmbH, Mannheim **Location** Berlin, Germany **Month / Year** June 2012 **Duration** Two days **Conception / Dramaturgy / Direction / Coordination / Graphics / Communication** insglück **Architecture** Atelier Bette **Lighting** Gahrens & Battermann GmbH **Catering** Hotel Berlin **Construction** I Point Dekorations- und Bühnenbau GmbH **Photos** insglück

# Volkswagen Service Forum 2012
## HAGEN INVENT

Location: Messe Berlin, Germany

Im April 2012 lud die Volkswagen AG ihre nationalen Serviceberater zu einer zentralen Motivations- und Schulungsveranstaltung nach Berlin ein, die als ganzheitliches Produkt- und Markenerlebnis konzipiert war.

In April 2012, Volkswagen AG invited its national service advisors to a key motivational and training event in Berlin, which was conceived as an integral product and brand experience.

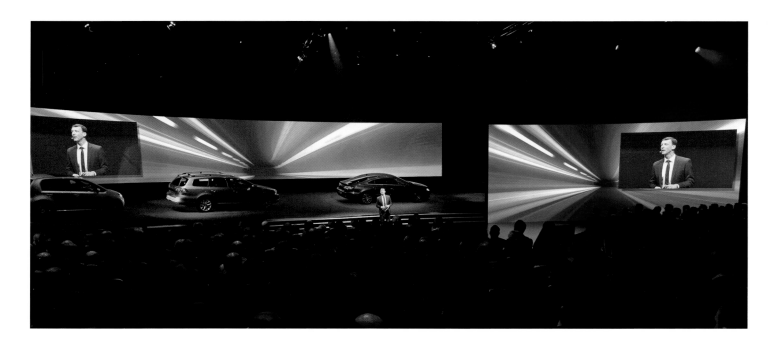

Ziel war es, das Selbstverständnis der Serviceberater als Markenbotschafter sowie ihre Markenbindung und Motivation zu steigern. Eine Kombination aus Fahrerlebnis, Businessmeeting, Abendveranstaltung und Schulungsmodul sollte die Begeisterung der Gäste für „ihre" Marke wecken.

Als zentraler Veranstaltungsort wurde in der Messe Berlin ein Markenraum geschaffen, der das Motto der Veranstaltung – „Mehr Puls. Mehr Drive." – in eine ebenso funktionale wie ästhetische Architektur übersetzte.

The objective was to improve service advisors' self-awareness as brand ambassadors and to strengthen their brand loyalty and motivation. A combination of driving experience, business meeting, evening event and training module was designed to awaken participants' enthusiasm for "their" brand.

A brand space was created in the main venue on the exhibition site of the Berlin Trade Fair, which translated the motto of the event – "More Pulse. More Drive." – into an attractive yet functional architecture.

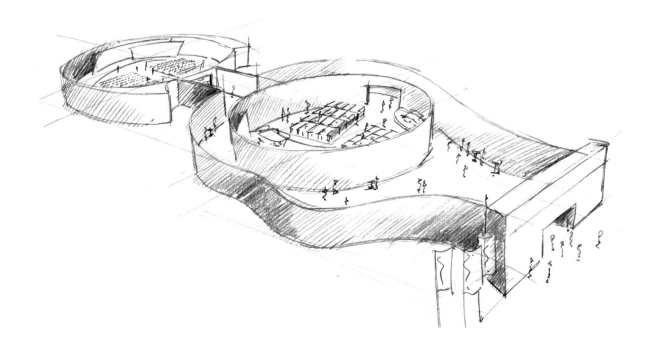

Ein gigantisches Portal, welches das Design des Key Visuals mit seinen markanten Fluchtlinien aufgriff, sog die Gäste förmlich in den Markenraum hinein. Dessen Inneres wurde von einem organischen Grundriss geprägt: Die Räume für Empfang und Lunch auf der einen sowie für Businessmeetings und Podiumsdiskussionen auf der anderen Seite wurden von einem dynamisch geschwungenen Wegesystem „umarmt".

So versetzte die Architektur die Gäste allzeit ins Zentrum des Geschehens; Antriebskraft und Dynamik waren in diesem den Dialog fördernden und zur Interaktion einladenden Veranstaltungsraum jederzeit spürbar.

A gigantic portal suggested by the design of the key visual with its striking vanishing points served to virtually draw guests into the brand space. Its interior was characterized by an organic layout: both the rooms for reception and lunch, as well as those for business meetings and panel discussions were "embraced" by a powerfully curving system of routes.

Accordingly, the architecture continually placed the guests at the center of things; drive and dynamism were perpetually palpable in this event space, encouraging both dialog and interaction.

**Agency** HAGEN INVENT GmbH & Co. KG, Düsseldorf **Client** Volkswagen AG, Wolfsburg **Location** Messe Berlin, Germany **Month / Year** April 2012 **Duration** 13 days **Conception / Dramaturgy / Direction / Coordination / Architecture / Graphics / Communication** HAGEN INVENT **Media** MPG Media Picture Group GmbH **Lighting** Neumann & Müller **Artists / Showacts** Yvi Quainoo **Catering** Capital Catering GmbH **Construction** Planwerkstatt GmbH **Photos** Bernhard Wiemann **Awards** Automotive Brand Contest 2012, Galaxy Award 2012, EuBEA Award 2012 (Best Incentive / Team Building); nominated: German Design Award 2013, BEA Award 2013, EuBEA Award 2012 (Best Internal Event / Convention)

# Neuroth Employee Days
## KOOP Live Marketing

Location: Dubrovnik, Croatia

Zum 105-jährigen Jubiläum der Neuroth AG lud der Hörgerätespezialist seine Mitarbeiter dazu ein, ein gemeinsames Erlebnis in urlaubsähnlicher Atmosphäre zu genießen. Die Reise nach Dubrovnik stand unter dem Slogan „Das Ohr unterscheidet tausende von Geräuschen – verpassen Sie nicht ein einziges!"

In celebration of its 105th anniversary, hearing aid specialist Neuroth AG invited its employees to join them on a company trip with a real vacation feel to it. The trip to Dubrovnik was given the motto "Our ears can discern thousands of sounds – don't miss a single one of them!"

Per Charterflug reisten rund 800 Mitarbeiter in die südkroatische Stadt Dubrovnik, wo die Geschäftsführung Ansprachen hielt und Neuroth-Partner Workshops veranstalteten. Außerdem lockten verschiedene Freizeitaktivitäten von Sport bis Entspannung sowie eine Stadterkundungstour. Eine Handvoll ausgewählter Journalisten begleitete das Unternehmen. Diese erhielten die Möglichkeit, Kamingespräche mit der Geschäftsführung zu führen sowie die neuesten technischen Produktentwicklungen kennen zu lernen.

Chartered flights whisked 800 employees down to the city of Dubrovnik in southern Croatia, where management held talks for the teams and organized Neuroth partner workshops. Furthermore, a range of leisure activities were offered rom sports to relaxation to a sightseeing tour through the city. A handful of selected journalists also accompanied the group and were given the opportunity to have one-on-ones with management and to find out more about the company's latest technical developments.

Um die einzelnen Sinne anzusprechen, gab es auf der Festung Revelin eine Laser-Show, deren Höhepunkte der Markenkommunikation dienten und die Neuroth-Werbebotschaften beinhalteten. Zudem fand ein Dinner im Dunkeln statt, das von Klaviermusik begleitet wurde. Dies sollte den Mitarbeitern näherbringen, dass viele Menschen mit Einschränkungen eines oder mehrerer Sinne leben müssen und die Philosophie von Neuroth darin besteht, diese Menschen zu unterstützen.

Appealing to each one of the senses, the Revelin fortress was also lit up in a laser show, its highlights also serving as a means of brand communication boasting Neuroth's advertising message. In addition, employees enjoyed a dinner in the dark with musical accompaniment on the piano. This was intended to give employees an experience of the sensorial limitations that many people have to live with; after all, Neuroth's philosophy is to provide such people with the support they need.

**Agency** KOOP Live Marketing GmbH & Co. KG, Vienna **Client** Neuroth AG, Graz **Location** Dubrovnik, Croatia **Month / Year** October 2012 **Duration** Three days **Concept / Dramaturgy / Coordination / Decoration / Graphics / Communication** KOOP Live Marketing **Films** Zwupp.Collective **Catering** Hotel Valamar Lacroma **Photos** Christian Kinza, Graz

# PUBLIC EVENT

# Montréal signs "Ode à la vie"
## Moment Factory

Location: Sagrada Família, Barcelona, Spain

Jedes Jahr lädt Barcelona eine ausländische Stadt als Gast zu ihrem Mercè Festival ein. 2012 fiel die Wahl auf Montréal. Das dort ansässige Multimedia- und Entertainmentstudio Moment Factory wurde beauftragt, eine Multimediashow zu entwerfen, die auf die berühmte Fassade der Sagrada Família projiziert wurde.

Every year the city of Barcelona invites a foreign city to its Mercè Festival. In 2012, Montréal was chosen. Its city elders commissioned Moment Factory, a Montréal-based multimedia and entertainment studio, to create a sound and light spectacle, which was projected onto the façade of one of the city's emblems: the Sagrada Família.

Antoni Gaudí, der Architekt der Sagrada Família, fertigte im Laufe seines Lebens eine ganze Reihe farbiger Entwurfsskizzen an, die seine Kathedrale in fertigem Zustand zeigen. Gaudís Begeisterung für die Formen der Natur und ihre Farben wurde so zur wichtigsten Inspirationsquelle für Design und Ablauf des Events. Dessen Erzählstruktur basierte auf den mystischen Aspekten der Basilika und war als Reverenz an die Schöpfungsgeschichte in sieben Akte unterteilt. „Ode à la vie" begann mit den Zeichnungen Gaudís und verwirklichte dann nach und nach seine Vision: seine Kirche in Farben zu sehen.

Die komplexe Fassade der Sagrada Família war bei weitem eine der anspruchsvollsten Oberflächen, die Moment Factory bislang zu bespielen hatte. Das Kreativstudio nutzte seine eigene Software (X-Agora) für das interaktive Medienmanagement und Playback sowie zur Gestaltung der gewölbten Bildersequenz auf der organischen, modularen Fassade der Basilika. Der multimediale Inhalt wurde zunächst auf einem digitalen 3D-Modell und sodann auf einer meterhohen Maquette getestet, bevor er schließlich auf die eigentliche Fassade modelliert wurde.

In the course of his life, Antoni Gaudí, the architect of the Sagrada Família, produced an entire series of colored design sketches showing the cathedral in its finished state. Gaudí's enthusiasm for natural shapes and their colors were the key source of inspiration for the design and course of the event. Its narrative structure was based on the mystical aspects of the basilica, and as an homage to the history of creation divided into seven acts. "Ode à la vie" began with Gaudì's drawings and then gradually realized his vision: of seeing his church in color.

The complex façade of the Sagrada Família was by far one of the most difficult surface that Moment Factory had to work with to date. The creative studio used its own software suite (X-Agora) for interactive media management and playback and in oder to make the images blend and bend on the organic and modular façade of the Basilica. The multimedia content was first tested on a 3D digital model, then on a meter high maquette before finally moulding itself to the actual façade.

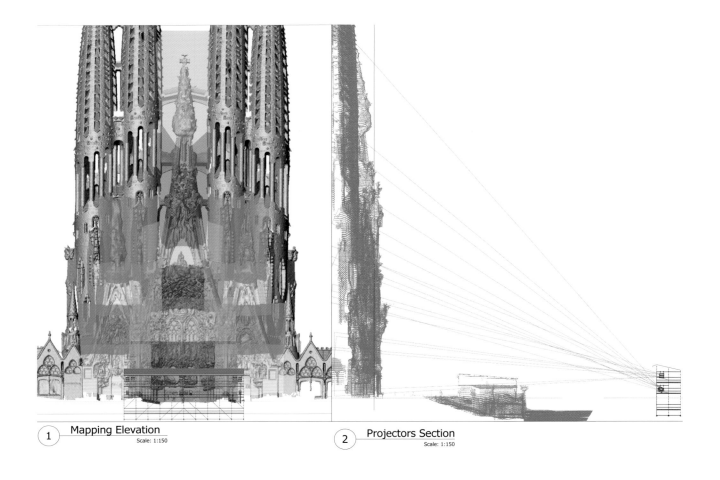

1 Mapping Elevation
Scale: 1:150

2 Projectors Section
Scale: 1:150

Mehr als 113.000 Zuschauer kamen zur Sagrada Família, um sich das Multimediaspektakel anzusehen. Das Projekt stieß auf lebhafte Resonanz in Blogs und Social Media – auch Filmaufnahmen fanden weite Verbreitung im Internet. Allein das Demovideo wurde im Laufe eines Monats auf 234 Webseiten vorgestellt und in insgesamt 147 Ländern über 190.000-mal angesehen.

Over 113,000 spectators at the site viewed the Sagrada Família multimedia spectacle and the project also featured hugely in blogs and social media – films were widely circulated on the Internet. In the course of a month the demo video alone was presented on 234 websites and was viewed by 190,000 people in over 147 nations.

**Agency** Moment Factory, Montréal **Client** City of Montréal **Location** Sagrada Família, Barcelona, Spain **Month / Year** September 2012 **Duration** Three days **Executive producers** Éric Fournier, Joanna Marsal **Multimedia director** Nelson de Robles **Scriptwriter** Mareike Lenhart **Creative director** Sakchin Bessette **Technology director** Dominic Audet **Creative collaborators** Dominic Champagne, Brigitte Poupart **Music composers** Anthony Rozankovic, Misteur Valaire **Lighting designer** Gabriel Pontbriand **Lighting engineer** Dominic Lemieux **Technical director** Alexis Bluteau **Original idea** Jaques Renaud (RENAUD – Architecture d'événements) **Projectionist** Francois David Gagnon **Sound designer** Jean-Michel Caron **Project coordinator** Geneviève Isabelle Michaud **Motion designers** Fabricio Lima, Charlotte Risch, Aude Guivarc'h, Adam Hummell **Graphic designers** Frederic Cordier, Joanna Czadowska, Gabo Gesualdi **Photos** Pep Daudé / Basílica Sagrada Família **Awards** GRAFIKA Award – Grand Prize for Interactive Installation, C2-MTL/Fast Company's "Creative Answers to commercial questions" – Multimedia

# BAMBI 2012
## DREINULL, Kimmig

Location: CCD Congress Center Düsseldorf, Germany

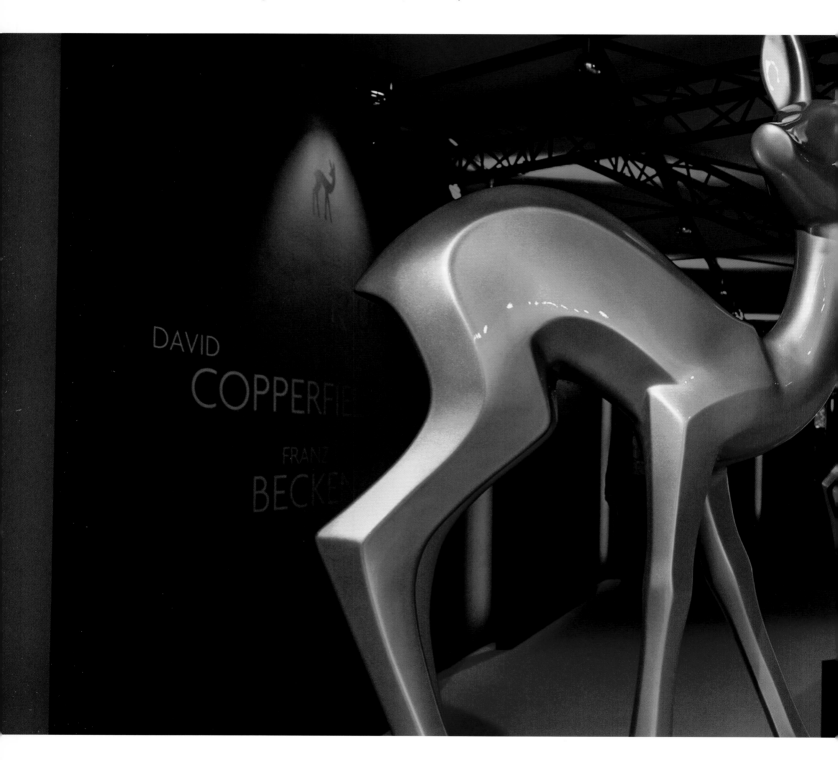

Der europäische Medienpreis „Bambi" blickt auf eine lange Tradition zurück; seit 1948 wird die Bambi-Gala von Hubert Burda Media ausgerichtet. Im Rahmen des Bühnendesigns für 2012 wurde Wert darauf gelegt, dass die Vergangenheit spürbar bleibt und gleichzeitig moderne Elemente das Set maßgeblich auffrischen.

The Bambi European Media Award has a long tradition, Hubert Burda Media having been organizing the Bambi gala since 1948. In conceiving the stage design for 2012, importance was attached to ensuring the past remained palpable, while using modern elements to infuse some pep into the set.

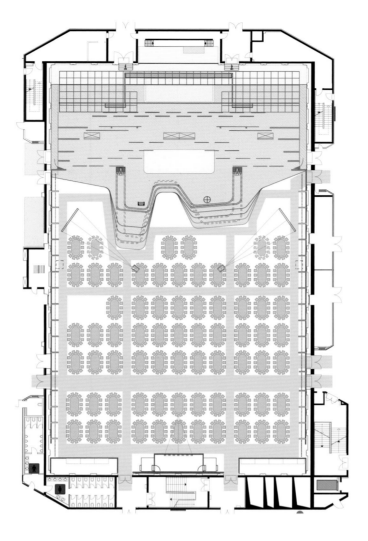

Die Farbgebung, bei der Gold- und Brauntöne domi-nierten und die die Außen- und Empfangsbereiche der Veranstaltung definierte, wurde auf der Bühne durch Vorhänge aus geschliffenen Glaskugeln ergänzt, die in verschiedenen Varianten bewegt werden konnten. In die Tiefe der Bühne gestaffelt waren insgesamt acht Ebenen angeordnet, über die neben den Glasvorhän-gen High-Res- und Low-Res-LED-Flächen bewegt und mit Videos bespielt wurden.

The color scheme, in which gold and brown tones pre-vailed, and which dominated the outdoor and reception areas, was complemented by curtains of cut-glass bau-bles, which could be moved in different variations. Eight levels were given a staggered arrangement across the depth of the stage, above which, alongside the glass cur-tains, high-res and low-res LED screens showed videos.

Der Gästebereich vor der Bühne wurde mit einem zusätzlichen LED-Band eingefasst, sodass die Gäste von einem 270°-Videopanorama umgeben waren. Dieses Set ermöglichte zahlreiche abwechslungsreiche Settings, in denen nationale und internationale Künstler wie Lady Gaga und Céline Dion bei ihren Auftritten effektvoll in Szene gesetzt wurden.

In front of the stage an additional LED strip enclosed the guest area, such that the guests were surrounded by a 270° video panorama. The set permitted numerous, diverse settings, in which national and international stars such as Lady Gaga and Céline Dion could be presented to great advantage during their performances.

**Agency** DREINULL Agentur für Mediatainment GmbH & Co. KG, Berlin; Kimmig Entertainment GmbH, Oberkirch **Client** Hubert Burda Media, Munich **Location** CCD Congress Center Düsseldorf, Germany **Month / Year** November 2012 **Duration** One day **Conception / Dramaturgy** Phillip Pröttel **Direction / Coordination** Utz Weber **Architecture** Olaf Schiefner **Graphics / Communication** SevenOne Media **Media** DREINULL Motion **Lighting** Jerry Appelt **Films** screen[worx] **Music / Artists / Showacts** Céline Dion, One Direction, Peter Maffay, Andreas Gabalier, Cro, Lady Gaga et al. **Construction / Decoration** WE make it **Catering** Käfer Catering **Photos** Ralf Rühmeier, Berlin

# Mercedes-Benz A-class Pavilion Roadshow
## LIGANOVA

Location: Several cities in 22 European countries

Um seine neue A-Klasse zu präsentieren, ließ Mercedes-Benz im vergangenen Jahr 16 Pavillons durch insgesamt 22 europäische Länder touren. 82 Mal wurden die Pavillons aufgebaut und dabei insgesamt rund 70.000 km zurückgelegt.

Last year, to present its new A-class, Mercedes-Benz had 16 pavilions tour through 22 European countries. The tour incorporated 82 stops and in all covered some 70,000 km.

Mit ihrem progressiven Design kommunizierten die Pavillons das neue Erscheinungsbild der Marke. Um neue Zielgruppen zu erschließen, wurden die Pavillons an zentralen Orten und ausgewählten Hotspots platziert. Im Zentrum der Roadshow stand hierbei die Fahrzeugpräsentation. Darüber hinaus weckten Infotainment, digitale Interaktionen und Probefahrten Interesse und Aufmerksamkeit der Besucher.

Die Pavillons waren modular gebaut und konnten sowohl im Innen- als auch im Außenbereich eingesetzt werden. Es gab zudem unterschiedlichste Modulvarianten, die flexibel kombinierbar waren, um auf jede Raumsituationen reagieren zu können. Zur Ausstattung gehörten neben stilvollen und zur Designwelt passenden Möbeln auch eine Vielzahl von Medienträgern.

With their advanced design the pavilions communicated the brand's new image. In order to attract new target groups the pavilions were installed in central locations and selected hot spots. The focus of the roadshow was always the presentation of the vehicle. In addition, infotainment, digital interactions and test drives served to capture visitors' interest and attention.

Thanks to their modular structure the pavilions could be set up both inside and outdoors. There were also a wide variety of modules that could be combined flexibly to suit the spatial situation. They featured numerous media and were furnished with stylish furniture in keeping with the design setting.

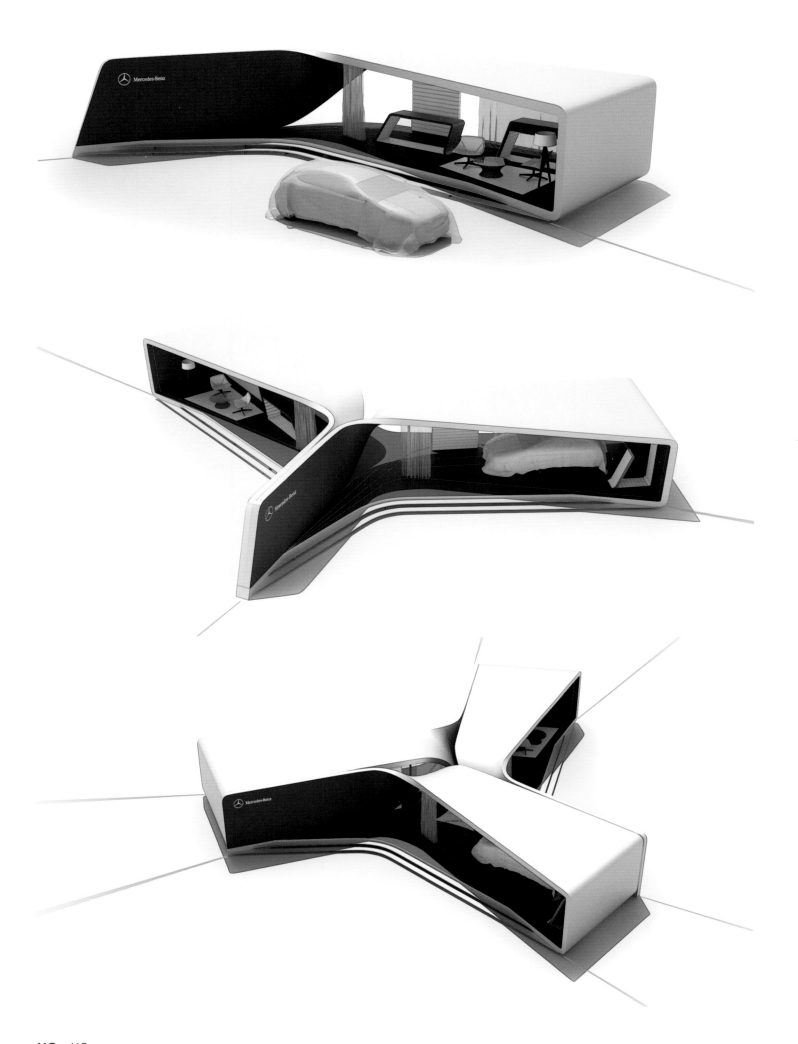

**Agency** LIGANOVA GmbH – The BrandRetail Company, Stuttgart **Client** Daimler AG, Stuttgart **Location** Several locations in 22 European countries **Month/Year** May–December 2012 **Duration** Eight months **Conception/Dramaturgy/Direction/Coordination/Architecture/Lighting** LIGANOVA GmbH **Graphics/Communication/Media** LIGANOVA GmbH, Jung von Matt AG **Music** LIGANOVA GmbH, Wolf & Dietz GbR **Artists/Showacts** Mercedes-Benz **Decoration** Daimler AG **Construction** Nüssli AG **Photos** LIGANOVA GmbH, Daimler AG

# Andrea Berg - The 20 Years Show
## DREINULL, Kimmig

Location: Messe Offenburg, Germany

Die Schlagersängerin Andrea Berg ist in der deutschen Musiklandschaft seit 20 Jahren eine feste Größe. Ihr Bühnenjubiläum war der Anlass für eine große Live-show in der ARD im Januar 2013.

The singer Andrea Berg has been a prominent figure in traditional German music for 20 years. In January 2013, she celebrated 20 years on stage with a major live show on ARD television.

Die Grundidee der Veranstaltung war, eine Nähe zwischen der Künstlerin und den Zuschauern sowie (prominenten) Weggefährten herzustellen. Eine große Galatreppe vor einer 34 m breiten LED-Wand führte auf eine zentrale Rundbühne, von der zwei langgezogene Catwalks abgingen – einer davon führte direkt ins Publikum, ein anderer zum Fanclub der Künstlerin.

Die Veranstaltung zeichnete sich durch eine zeitgemäße Gestaltung und den Einsatz moderner Technik aus und setzte sich damit von bekannten Schlagerklischees ab. Als optisches Highlight diente eine schwebende Korona aus Versatubes. Viele bekannte Musiker aus dem deutschsprachigen Raum sowie Lionel Ritchie komplettierten die bunte Show durch ihre Auftritte.

The basic idea behind the event was to create a closeness between the artist and the audience and (famous) colleagues. A large gala staircase in front of a 34 m wide LED screen led to a central, round stage, with two long catwalks leading from it – one directly into the audience, the other to the artist's fan club.

A contemporary design and the use of cutting-edge technology characterized the event, serving to distance the show from familiar pop clichés. A suspended corona of versa tubes provided a visual highlight. Performances by many well-known musicians from German-speaking countries, as well as Lionel Ritchie, rounded out the colorful show.

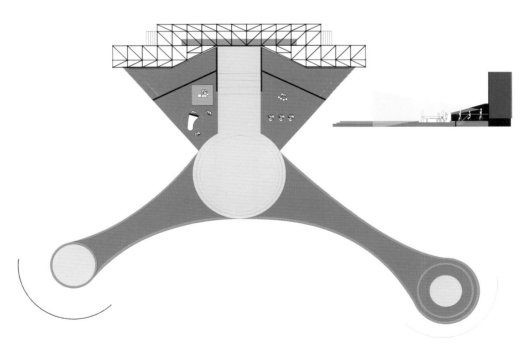

**Agency** DREINULL Agentur für Mediatainment GmbH & Co. KG, Berlin **Client** Kimmig Entertainment GmbH, Oberkirch
**Location** Messe Offenburg, Germany; ARD **Month / Year** January 2013 **Duration** One day **Conception / Dramaturgy** Marion Gaedicke, Alexander Semjow **Direction / Coordination** Ladislaus Kiraly **Architecture** Thomas Barnstedt, Act in common **Graphics / Communications** Ferber Management, MDR **Media** flora&faunavisions **Lighting** Manfred "Ollie" Olma
**Music** Andrea Berg et al. **Artists / Showacts** DJ Bobo, DJ Ötzi, Andreas Gabalier, Roland Kaiser, Pur, Lionel Ritchie et al.
**Decoration / Construction** Studio Hamburg **Photos** Meiko Janke, Berlin

# Urban Age: Electric City 2012
## TRIAD Berlin

Location: The Circus Space, London, UK

Im Rahmen der Urban-Age-Konferenzreihe der Alfred Herrhausen Gesellschaft wurden Fragen zur Vernetzung und Elektrifizierung von Städten und die Folgen für die Urbanisierung unter besonderem Fokus auf innovativen und grünen Technologien diskutiert.

As part of the series of Urban Age conferences organized by the Alfred Herrhausen Society participants discussed issues relating to the networking and electrification of cities and the consequences for urbanization, with a special focus on innovative and green energies.

Rund 300 Vertreter aus Politik, Wirtschaft und Forschung kamen zum zweitägigen Event im Dezember 2012 nach London. Die Konferenz fand im ehemaligen Elektrizitätswerk der „Electric Light Station" statt, das sich aufgrund seiner früheren Nutzung als architektonische Allegorie des Konferenzthemas präsentierte.

Around 300 representatives from the fields of politics, business and research attended the two-day event in December 2012 in London. The venue, Shoreditch "Electric Light Station", was once an electricity generating station, making it an apt architectural allegory of the conference topic.

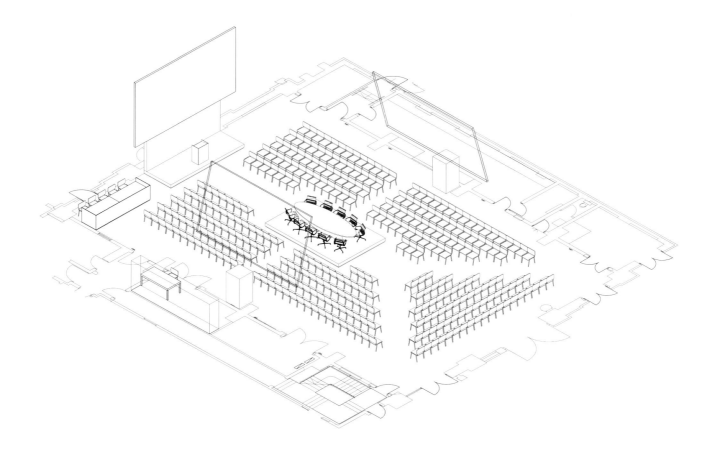

Die Gestaltung orientierte sich am übergreifenden Thema „Urban Age" und am Diskussionsschwerpunkt „Vernetzung der wachsenden Städte und deren Elektrifizierung": Das Grundelement bildete das Gebäude, dessen rohes Ziegelmauerwerk mit einer bewusst minimalistischen Kombination aus Licht und Projektionen medial effektvoll inszeniert wurde. Lichtakzente im Veranstaltungsdesign bildeten einen visuellen Kontrast zum lichtlosen Raum. Projizierte urbane Motive komplementierten das Thema der Verstädterung und holten es in das Setting. Die mittige Positionierung der Redner und des Panels erzeugte eine konzentrierte Konferenzatmosphäre, die zur Partizipation einlud.

Auch die anschließende Abendveranstaltung für geladene Gäste im Londoner Restaurant „The Wapping Project", das ehemals als Hydraulikwerk der Tower Bridge diente, griff erneut das Konferenzthema auf.

The design was inspired by the overarching topic "Urban Age" and the focal discussion topic "Networking of urban agglomerations and their electrification". The building formed the main element with a deliberately minimalistic staging of its rough-plastered brickwork using a combination of light and projections, to great effect. Light accents in the event design created a visual contrast to the unlit space. Projections of urban motifs complemented the topic of urbanization and drew it into the setting. The central positioning of the speakers and panel generated a focused conference atmosphere which invited participation.

The evening event for invited guests at the London restaurant "The Wapping Project", which was previously the hydraulic power station for Tower Bridge, continued the theme of the conference.

**Agency** TRIAD Berlin Projektgesellschaft mbH, Berlin **Client** Alfred Herrhausen Society – The international Forum of Deutsche Bank mbH, Berlin **Location** The Circus Space, London, UK **Month / Year** December 2012 **Duration** Two days **Concept / Dramaturgy / Direction / Coordination / Architecture / Decoration** TRIAD **Graphics / Communication** Atelier Works, London **Media** London School of Economics **Lighting** Neumann & Müller GmbH, Speirs & Major **Catering** Food Show Ltd., London **Construction** Plan 2 **Photos** Paul Clarke, Merstham

# EXHIBITION, CONSUMER EVENT

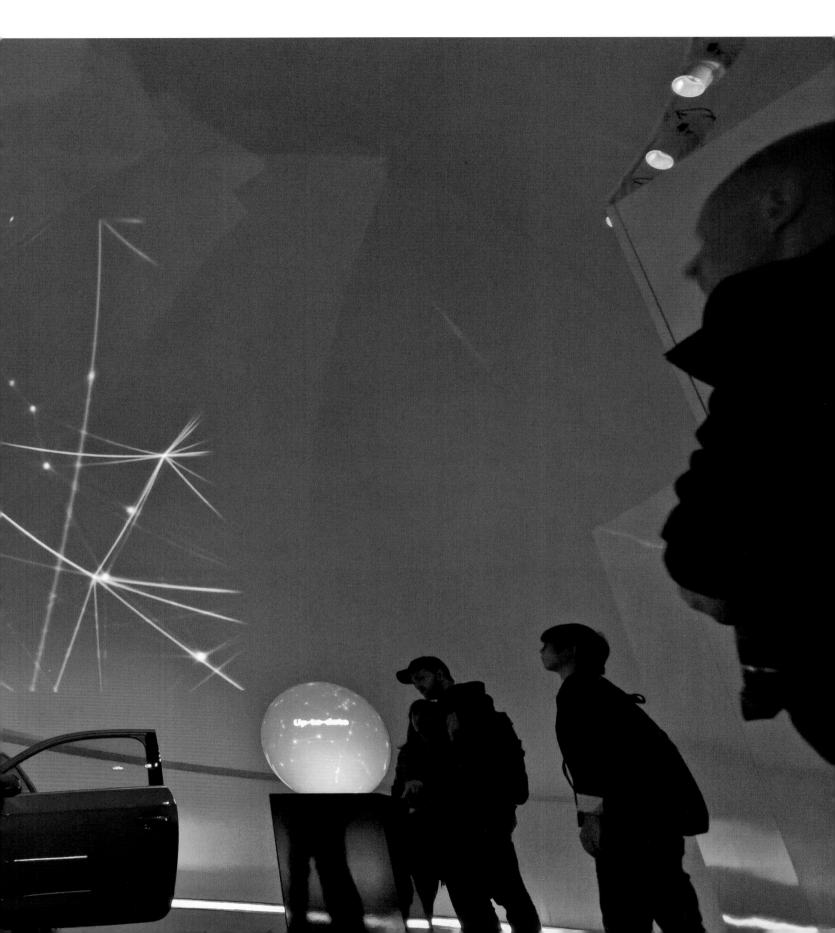

# Magnum Infinity Lounge Hamburg
## east end communications

Location: Hamburg, Germany, and several other locations in Europe

Persönliche Glücksmomente mit dem Premiumeis Magnum konnten die Besucher der Magnum Infinity Lounge Hamburg im Sommer 2012 erleben.

Visitors to the Magnum Infinity Lounge Hamburg were able to experience personal moments of happiness with the premium ice-cream, Magnum, in the summer of 2012.

Anlass für die Einrichtung der Hamburger Magnum Infinity Lounge war der Launch der Premiummarke Magnum Infinity. Die mit dem Konzept des Pop-up-Stores einhergehende Vergänglichkeit passte dabei hervorragend zu dem zeitlich limitierten Premiumeis. Die Idee zu diesem temporären Eis-Erlebnis kommt von der Londoner Agentur Hot Pickle; Die Agentur für Live-Kommunikation east end communications war für die Gesamtkonzeption und Umsetzung in Deutschland verantwortlich.

The Magnum Infinity Lounge was created especially to launch the premium brand Magnum Infinity. The idea of transience connected with the pop-up store went excellently with the fact that the premium ice was only available for a limited period of time. The concept for this temporary ice-cream experience came from the London agency Hot Pickle, while the agency for live communication, east end communications, was responsible for the overall concept und realization in Germany.

Das Design der Magnum Infinity Lounge, bei dem die Farben Braun und Beige dominierten, war an das bekannte Stiel-Eis angelehnt. Es bot somit die perfekte Umgebung, um sich für eiskalte Kreationen inspirieren zu lassen.

Der Pop-up-Store hatte im Sommer 2012 für zweieinhalb Wochen seine Türen auf über 290 m² inmitten bester Innenstadtlage in Hamburg geöffnet. Weitere Locations der Magnum Infinity Lounge waren Paris, London, Istanbul und São Paulo.

The design of the Magnum Infinity Lounge in which the colors brown and beige dominated, was inspired by the well-known ice cream. As such, it offered a perfect setting to get inspiration for ice-cold creations.

Covering over 290 m² and located in a prime inner-city location, the Hamburg Magnum Infinity Lounge opened its doors for two and a half weeks in summer 2012. Paris, London, Istanbul and São Paulo were amongst the other locations of the Magnum Infinity Lounge.

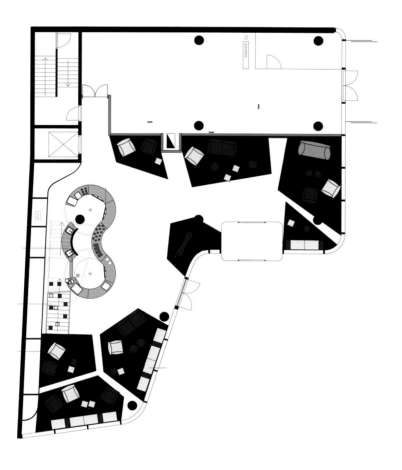

Wer sich hier ein ganz persönliches Geschmackserlebnis schaffen wollte, konnte an der Magnum Infinity Bar einen Eiskern in flüssige Schokolade tauchen und ihn mit den eigenen Lieblingszutaten bestreuen. Von prominenter Seite exklusiv kreierte Magnum-Infinity-Varianten dienten dabei als Inspiration. Das Ergebnis konnte auf der Magnum-Genusswand als eigene Notiz und als Anregung für andere dokumentiert werden.

For those seeking a highly individual taste experience it was possible to dip a Magnum ice-cream into molten chocolate at the Magnum Infinity Bar and cover it with your own favorite topping. Magnum Infinity variations created exclusively by top names served as inspiration. The final product could be posted on the Magnum enjoyment wall as a reminder note for the creator, or as inspiration for others.

**Agency** east end communications GmbH, Hamburg **Client** Unilever Deutschland Holding GmbH, Hamburg **Location** Hamburg, Germany, and several other locations in Europe **Month / Year** July 2012 **Duration** Two and a half weeks **Concept / Dramaturgy** Hot Pickle **Dramaturgy / Direction / Coordination / Architecture / Construction** east end communications **Catering** Unilever Deutschland Holding **Photos** Ulrich Lindenthal, Hamburg

# Schwarzkopf "Lightbox by Karl Lagerfeld"
## zet:project.

Location: Graf-Adolf-Platz, Düsseldorf, Germany

Im Jahr 2011 plante Schwarzkopf im Zuge seiner offiziellen Beauty-Partnership und seines Sponsorings des European Song Contests einen aufmerksamkeitsstarken Öffentlichkeitsauftritt. Ziel war es, ein Consumer Event zu kreieren, das Raum für eine erlebnisgestützte Marken- und Produktbegegnung ermöglichte.

In 2011 as part of its official beauty partnership and sponsoring of the European Song Contest, Schwarzkopf planned a highly attention-grabbing public appearance. The objective: to create a consumer event providing scope for a product and brand encounter supported by events.

Die Schwarzkopf „Lightbox by Karl Lagerfeld" garantierte als vom Stardesigner eigens entworfenes, temporäres Gebäude eine geeignete Umgebung für ein öffentlichkeitswirksames und hochwertiges Beratungs- und Lifestyleangebot. Die 10 m hohe Lightbox präsentierte sich in zeitgenössischem Design und bot auf rund 300 m² einen interaktiven Mix aus Produkterlebniscenter, Salon, Café und Verkauf. In vier Wochen fanden insgesamt über 14.000 Besucher den Weg zu dem temporären Bau in der Nähe der Düsseldorfer Königsallee.

As a temporary building conceived by the star designer himself, the Schwarzkopf "Lightbox by Karl Lagerfeld" delivered a suitable setting for high-quality advisory and lifestyle offers that made for excellent publicity. Covering around 300 m² and with a contemporary design, the 10 m high Lightbox offered an interactive mix of product experience center, salon, café and sales outlet. In four weeks over 14,000 people visited the temporary building near the prestigious Königsallee in Düsseldorf.

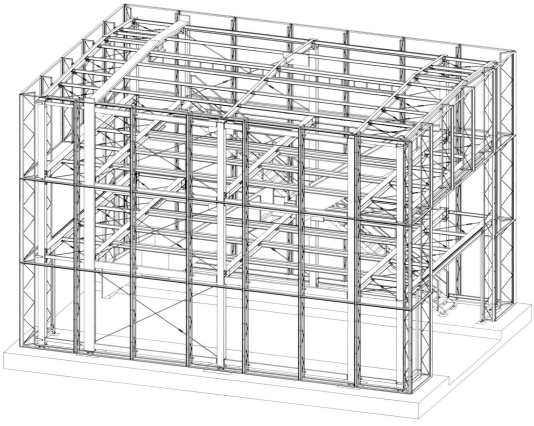

Durch die geschickte Standortwahl, die einzigartige Architektur und die nächtliche Illumination fügte sich die Lightbox als Gesamtkunstwerk in die Innenstadt ein. Dieses ansprechende Ambiente wurde auch für Abendevents genutzt. Eine große Medienwirksamkeit wurde durch das Bespielen aller relevanten Kanäle und Formate – von Print und TV bis hin zu einem eigenen Youtube-Channel und offiziellen Facebook-Seiten – erreicht.

Thanks to the clever choice of location, unique architecture and night-time illumination the Lightbox fitted well into the downtown area as a multi-media happening. The attractive venue was also used for evening events. And by featuring it in all relevant channels and formats from print and TV through to a special YouTube channel and official Facebook pages, a high degree of publicity was achieved.

**Agency** zet:project.GmbH, Leinfelden-Echterdingen **Client** Henkel AG & Co. KGaA, Düsseldorf **Location** Graf-Adolf-Platz, Düsseldorf, Germany **Month / Year** April–May 2011 **Duration** One month **Concept / Dramaturgy / Graphics / Communication** Henkel **Direction / Coordination / Artists / Showacts / Decoration** zet:project. **Architecture** HPP Hentrich-Petschnigg & Partner GmbH & Co. KG **Lighting** zet:project., BKSF GmbH **Catering** Henkel Business Gastronomie **Construction** BKSF GmbH **Photos** Jack Kulke, Stefan Krempl **Awards** Consumer Event EVA Award (gold)

# eBay Store Berlin
## east end communications

Location: Berlin, Germany

Mit einem 400 m² großen temporären Pop-up-Store in Berlin-Mitte inszenierte der Online-Marktplatz eBay das Thema Weihnachtsshopping einmal offline. Besucher konnten zehn Tage lang in ruhiger und entspannter Atmosphäre ihre Weihnachtseinkäufe erledigen – mit dem Smartphone und per QR-Code.

The online marketplace eBay recently created an offline presentation on the theme of Christmas shopping in the form of a 400 m² pop-up store in Berlin's Mitte district. For ten days, visitors were able to do their Christmas shopping in a quiet, peaceful atmosphere – using nothing more than their smartphones and the QR codes given.

Die Verbindung zwischen Online- und Offline-Handel wurde im Kaufraum erlebbar: 150 reale Produkte konnten begutachtet und anschließend durch das Scannen eines QR-Codes mit dem Smartphone online bei eBay gekauft werden. Im Anschluss an die Weihnachtstage wurde der Laden umgebaut – nun konnten die Kunden Geschenke-Flops oder doppelt erhaltene Präsente vor Ort fotografieren, beschreiben und schließlich bei eBay einstellen.

Der Pop-up-Store gab einen Eindruck davon, wie eBay und PayPal mit ihren Technologien die Gegenwart und Zukunft des Handels mitgestalten. So wurde den Besuchern ein Blick auf die Frage ermöglicht, wie die Menschen in den nächsten Jahren einkaufen und bezahlen werden. Die Besucher konnten vor Ort das Wohnzimmer, das Café und die Modeboutique von morgen erleben.

The outlet rendered the connection between online and offline trade truly tangible: 150 products were on display for visitors to take a look at and then with a quick scan and a few swipes on their smartphone screen they could buy them online at eBay. Once the Christmas holidays had passed the store was revamped into a hub where people take their unwanted or doubled-up gifts, photograph them, write their descriptions and put them up for auction online.

The pop-up store gave visitors an impression of how eBay and PayPal are shaping both the present and the future of online trading with their innovative technologies. As such, visitors were afforded a glimpse into the future: How will people shop and indeed pay in the coming years? Visitors could also try out the living room, café and fashion boutique of tomorrow.

Durch die Doppelnutzung wurden zwei nacheinander „aufpoppende" Läden geschaffen, die innerhalb der ersten 24 Stunden über 1.000 Besucher anlockten. Darüber hinaus erschienen in den ersten drei Tagen über 550 Medienstories, die für zusätzliche Aufmerksamkeit sorgten: im nationalen TV, Tageszeitungen und Newsportalen bis hin zu Blogs, Facebook und Instagram.

The double-purpose initiative created two very distinct stores, each "popping up" one after another, and drawing more than 1,000 visitors in the first 24 hours. Furthermore, more than 500 items of press coverage appeared in the first three days, which drews for even more public attention: from national TV stations and news portals to blogs, Facebook and Instagram.

**Agency** east end communications GmbH, Hamburg **Client** eBay GmbH, Europarc Dreilinden **Location** Berlin, Germany **Month / Year** December 2012 **Duration** One and a half weeks **Concept / Dramaturgy / Architecture / Construction** east end communications **Direction / Coordination / Graphics / Communication** east end communications, Achtung PR **Photos** eBay

# Cross-over-Event Audi Sphere 2012
## SCHMIDHUBER, KMS BLACKSPACE

Location: Christiansborg palace square, Copenhagen, Denmark

Mit einer temporären öffentlichen Präsentation zum Thema „Vorsprung durch Technik" ermöglichte Audi im Sommer 2012 Einblicke in die nachhaltige Mobilität der Zukunft.

With a temporary public presentation on the slogan "Advancement through technology" in summer 2012, Audi gave people a glimpse of sustainable mobility in the future.

Aufbereitet wurde das Thema in der „Audi Sphere" –
einem spektakulären Gebilde aus drei miteinander
verbundenen, begehbaren Kugelkörpern – auf dem
Schlossplatz Christiansborg, mitten im historischen
Stadtkern von Kopenhagen. Als mit Luft gefüllte
Baukörper bestanden die Kugeln aus einer leichten
PVC-Membran und verbildlichten somit nicht nur das
Thema Leichtbau, sondern wurden selbst zum Expo-
nat: Im Inneren jeder Kugel konnten die Besucher
je eine Themenwelt von Audi erforschen.

The topic was showcased in the "Audi Sphere" – a
spectacular structure of three inter-connected, walk-
through orbs – on Schlossplatz Christiansborg, in the
middle of Copenhagen's historical downtown. Volumes
filled with air and made of a light PVC membrane, the
orbs consequently not only visualized the topic of
lightweight construction but also acted as exhibits:
Visitors could explore a single Audi theme world inside
each one of them.

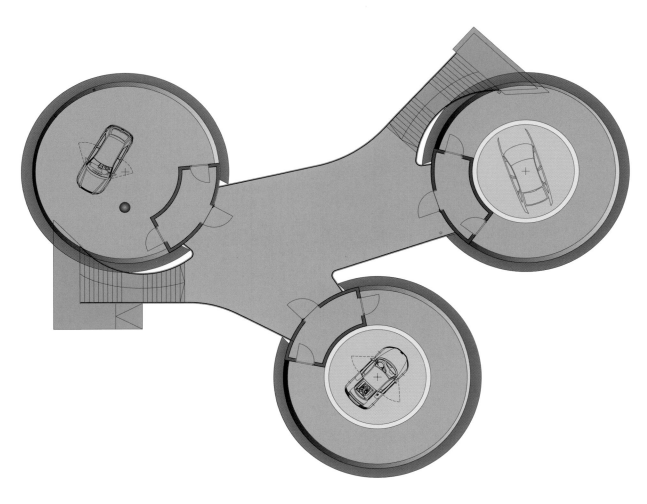

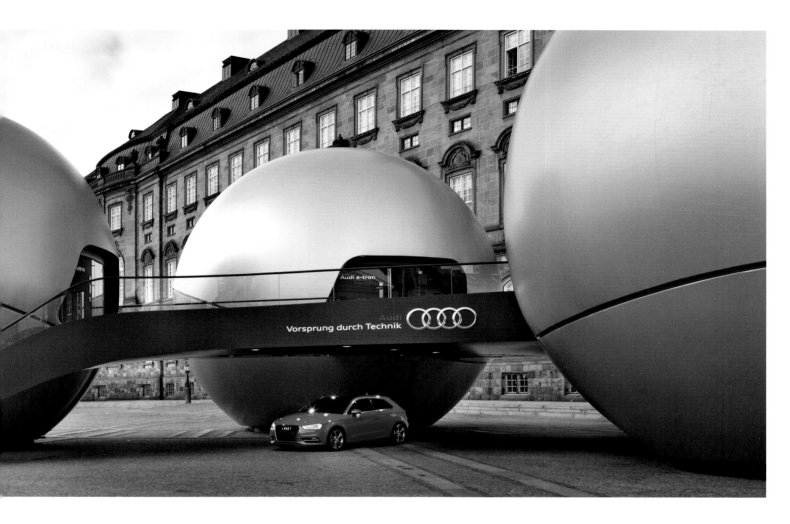

In der Kugel „Audi connect" erfuhren die Besucher alles über die Vernetzung des Fahrens. Mit der „Puffer Sphere", einer interaktiven Kugel, konnten sie eine 360°-Bespielung steuern und deren Inhalte vertiefen.

Die Leichtbautechnologien von Audi wurden in der Kugel „Audi ultra" präsentiert. Ein beweglicher Negativ-Scanner umlief einen Spaceframe im Zentrum des Raums und vervollständigte das Bild zu einem kompletten Fahrzeug. Kurze Texte informierten über die einzelnen Leichtbauteile und die Gewichtsersparnis, die sie ermöglichen.

Die Kugel „Audi e-tron" schließlich war dem Thema elektrische Mobilität gewidmet. 25 Windräder und ein in der Mitte des Raums platziertes e-tron-Fahrzeug animierten die Besucher zur aktiven Teilnahme: Durch Pusten setzten sich die Windräder in Bewegung und luden das Fahrzeug symbolhaft auf. Die roten LED-Lichter veranschaulichten den komplexen Zusammenhang zwischen sauberer Energiegewinnung und nachhaltigem Antrieb.

In the "Audi connect" sphere visitors discovered everything about networking driving. With the interactive "Puffer Sphere", they could control a 360° presentation and consolidate the information.

Audi's lightweight construction technologies were presented in the "Audi ultra" sphere. A moving negative scanner circulated a spaceframe in the center of the room and completed the image to create a complete vehicle. Short texts provided information about the individual lightweight components and the saving in weight they enable.

Finally, the "Audi e-tron" sphere was devoted to the topic of electric mobility. Some 25 wind turbines and an e-tron vehicle located in the center of the room encouraged visitors to become actively involved: Blowing set the turbines in motion, and charged the vehicle. The red LED lights visualized the complex connection between generating clean energy and sustainable propulsion.

Das Konzept der „Audi Sphere" wurde schon im März 2012 mit einer neuentwickelten Dauerausstellung in Wolfsburg präsentiert und bei dem Cross-over-Event in Kopenhagen wiederaufgegriffen: Jedem Besucher wurde eine personalisierbare interaktive Kugel in die Hand gegeben, mit der er Inhalte aktivieren und Informationen auswählen konnte.

The "Audi Sphere" concept was first staged in March 2012 with a newly-developed permanent exhibition in Wolfsburg, and elaborated on at the cross-over event in Copenhagen: Every visitor was given a personalized interactive sphere with which he or she could activate content and select information.

**Agency** SCHMIDHUBER, Munich; KMS BLACKSPACE, Munich **Client** AUDI AG, Ingolstadt **Location** Christiansborg palace square, Copenhagen, Denmark **Month / Year** July–August 2012 **Duration** Three weeks **Concept / Architecture** SCHMID-HUBER **Concept / Communication** KMS BLACKSPACE **Interaction** KOLLISION, Aarhus **Construction** A & A Expo International B. V., MT Wijk bij, Duurstede **Photos** Andreas Keller, Altdorf **Awards** iF communication design award 2013

# CHARITY, SOCIAL, CULTURAL EVENT

# Commemoration of the 8<sup>th</sup> Centenary of the Cathedral of Santiago de Compostela

## ACCIONA PRODUCCIONES Y DISEÑO

Location: Cathedral of Santiago de Compostela, Spain

Im Sommer 2011 verwandelte sich die Fassade der Kathedrale von Santiago de Compostela kurzzeitig in einen Traum aus Farben und magischen Bildern. Mit einer technisch innovativen 3D-Projektion ließ man die über 800-jährige Geschichte der Kathedrale Revue passieren.

In the summer of 2011 the façade of the Cathedral of Santiago de Compostela was temporarily transformed with a play of wonderful colors and attractive images. The cathedral's 800 year history was related in a technically sophisticated 3D projection.

Anlässlich des 800. Geburtstags der Kathedrale von Santiago de Compostela verwandelte die Agentur APD Events die Fassade in eine gewaltige Leinwand. Projektionen, Geräusche und Musik sowie ein Feuerwerk und zahlreiche Special Effects erweckten die Geschichte der weltberühmten Kirche zum Leben. Die Präsentation war als eine Abfolge historischer Episoden angelegt, die der Dramaturgie der musikalischen Untermalung folgte – Momente der Stille, plötzliche Ausbrüche und schließlich, als Höhepunkt, ein Feuerwerk.

To mark the 8th centenary of the Cathedral of Santiago de Compostela the agency APD Events transformed its façade into a huge projection screen. The history of the world-famous church was brought to life with projections, sounds and music, not to mention a firework display and numerous special effects. The presentation was composed as a sequence of historical episodes, with the drama of the musical accompaniment being followed by moments of silence, sudden outbursts and finally as a climax, a firework display.

Die Show ging zurück bis zu den Ursprüngen der Stadt und ihrer Kirche, welche eng mit dem Leben und Wirken des Heiligen Jakob verknüpft sind. So wurde das Bauwerk bildlich zerstört und anschließend wiedererrichtet, um die Entwicklung der Kathedrale im Laufe der Jahrhunderte nachzuzeichnen. Auch auf die Geschichte des Jakobswegs und der zahlreichen Kirchen, die ihn säumen, wurde eingegangen. Die Rundreise endete schließlich wieder in Santiago de Compostela und fand mit der virtuellen Rekonstruktion der heutigen barocken Fassade und einem effektgeladenen Blick ins Innere der Kirche ihren spektakulären Abschluss.

Abgerundet wurde das Event durch die „Zeitmaschine" – einem interaktiven Multimedia-Display mit Touchscreen, das den Besuchern erlaubte, einzelne Szenen der Show auszuwählen und abzuspielen. Das Event erregte großes Aufsehen in den Medien und Filmaufnahmen des Ereignisses fanden weite Verbreitung im Internet.

The show extended back to the origins of the town and its cathedral, which are closely linked with the life and work of St. Jacob. In order to trace the cathedral's development over the centuries the images showed its destruction and subsequent reconstruction. The narration also went into the history of the pilgrimage route, Jacob's Path, and the numerous churches lining its route. The tour ended in Santiago de Compostela coming to a spectacular conclusion with the virtual reconstruction of the current baroque façade and an insight, packed with special effects, into the church's interior.

The event was rounded out by a "time machine" – an interactive multimedia display with touch screen allowing visitors to select and play individual scenes of the show. It aroused great interest in the media, and many films of the event circulated on the Internet.

Es war weltweit das erste Mal, dass Video-Mapping auf einer barocken Fassade zur Anwendung kam. Bislang wurde Mapping nur auf flachen Oberflächen realisiert. Mit Hilfe der Warping-Technik, die die Projektion der Oberfläche wie eine zweite Haut anpasst, war es jedoch möglich, eine Bespielung zu entwerfen, die für die unregelmäßige Fassade der Kathedrale praktisch maßgeschneidert war.

This was the first time video-mapping had been used on a baroque façade. Previously, mapping could only be realized on flat surfaces. However, image warping fits the projection onto the surface like a second skin making it possible to create a show that was practically tailored to the irregular façade of the cathedral.

**Agency** ACCIONA PRODUCCIONES Y DISEÑO (Events), Madrid **Client** Consortium of Santiago de Compostela **Location** Cathedral of Santiago de Compostela, Spain **Month/Year** July 2011 **Duration** Eight days **Concept/Dramaturgy** Javier Sánchez, Miguel-Anxo Murado **Direction/Coordination** Javier Sánchez, Oscar Testón **Production** Juan Antonio Aranda, Libertad Dominguez **Architecture** Diana Jusdado **Audiovisual Programming** José Lerma **Films** Ivan Dominguez, Gustavo Calo, Mario Jiménez **Graphics/Communication** Elena Muñoz, Vicky Martín **Media** Luisa Gómez, Vicky Martín **Photos** ACCIONA PRODUCCIONES Y DISEÑO (Events) **Awards** European Best Event Awards: Best Cultural Event and 3rd European Best Event; Eventoplus Awards: Best Event of the Year

# Future without Hunger
## KOOP Live Marketing

Location: Aula der Wissenschaften, Vienna, Austria

Der international ausgerichtete Kongress „Hunger und nachhaltige Ernährungssicherheit" sollte das Bewusstsein für diese Themen in der Öffentlichkeit erhöhen. Dafür wurden in einem zweitägigen Event publikumswirksame Aktionen und kleinere Veranstaltungen in der Aula der Wissenschaften in Wien abgehalten.

The international congress "Global Hunger and Sustainable Food Security" was designed to raise public awareness of these topics. In a two-day event, actions aimed at garnering public attention and smaller events were held in the Aula der Wissenschaften in Vienna.

Rund 700 Teilnehmer aus aller Welt versammelten sich an zwei Tagen in Wien, um Vorträgen und Diskussionen mit Vertretern aus Politik, Wirtschaft, Kirche, Wissenschaft und Hilfsorganisationen zu neuen strategischen Ansätzen zur Ernährungssicherheit beizuwohnen. Dabei wurde das Gesagte in die Sprachen der Teilnehmer simultanübersetzt und zugleich komplett via Live-Stream im Internet übertragen. Das Saalpublikum war zum Mitdiskutieren aufgerufen.

Für eine ausreichende Themenpräsenz in der Öffentlichkeit sorgten nicht nur die geladenen Journalisten, sondern auch mehrere Side-Events wie beispielsweise der „Hunger-Demozug" in der Wiener Innenstadt, eine Themenschwerpunktwoche im ORF, die gemeinsame Messe im Stephansdom sowie ein Benefiz-Konzert im Museumsquartier in Wien.

Ein eigens eingerichteter Youtube-Channel („future without hunger") fasste noch einmal die wichtigsten Vorträge und Diskussionsbeiträge in Form von Kurzvideos zusammen. Mit dem Ziel, engagierte Menschen in Österreich, politische Entscheidungsträger, international tätige Unternehmen, NGOs sowie Wissenschaftler zusammenzuführen, erzielte „Zukunft ohne Hunger" national wie auch international eine außerordentliche Themenpräsenz. Dass nicht ausschließlich hinter verschlossenen Türen diskutiert wurde, leistete dazu einen wesentlichen Beitrag.

Some 700 participants from all over the world convened for two days in Vienna to attend lectures and discussions with representatives from politics, business, the church, science and relief organizations on new strategic approaches to food security. All spoken content was simultaneously translated into the participants' languages and broadcasted as a live stream on the Internet. The audience was encouraged to get involved in the discussions.

An adequate media presence was not only ensured through the journalists invited, but also several side events: among other things there was a demonstration against hunger in downtown Vienna, for a week Austrian news channel ORF aired a special series of programs devoted to the topic, a mass was held in St. Stephen's Cathedral, and there was a charity concert in Vienna's museum district.

A specially installed YouTube channel ("future without hunger") summarized the most important lectures and discussions in the guise of short videos. "Future without hunger" achieved extraordinary media presence both in Austria and abroad with the aim of mobilizing committed persons in Austria, political decision-makers, companies with international operations, NGOs and academics. The fact that discussions did not take place solely behind closed doors was highly instrumental in this respect.

**Agency** KOOP Live Marketing GmbH & Co. KG, Vienna **Client** Caritas Österreich, Vienna **Location** Aula der Wissenschaften, Vienna, Austria **Month / Year** June 2012 **Duration** Two days **Concept / Dramaturgy / Direction / Coordination / Graphics / Communication / Decoration** KOOP Live Marketing **Lighting / Films** Steiner Mediensysteme **Catering** CCP **Photos** Christian Müller, Vienna

# 175 Years of Mainzer Carneval-Verein
## Industrial Theater

Location: Palace of the Counts Elector, Mainz, Germany

Das 175. Vereinsjubiläum nahm der Mainzer Carneval-Verein 1838 e.V. zum Anlass, die Eröffnung der Kampagne 2012/2013 mit einem besonderen Ereignis zu feiern: am 11.11.2012 wurde im Kurfürstlichen Schloss von Mainz während der Auftaktveranstaltung nach 13 Jahren erstmals wieder ein Prinzenpaar gekürt.

The Mainz Carnival Association decided to celebrate its 175th anniversary by launching its 2012/2013 campaign with something really special: On November 11, 2012, during the opening event of the carnival period in the Palace of the Counts Elector in Mainz, a carnival prince and princess were chosen for the first time in 13 years.

Die Herausforderung für den Performance-Designer
und Regisseur Enno-Ilka Uhde bestand darin, traditio-
nelle und protokollarische Elemente der Kampagnen-
eröffnung des Mainzer Karnevals mit einer modernen
Inszenierung, die die Einbindung von Performance-
elementen und externen Künstlern vorsah, zu verknüpfen. So wurden der Einmarsch der ca. 70 Gardisten
und des Prinzenpaars, der feierliche Kürungsakt sowie
die verschiedenen Reden und Laudationes in ein Gesamtkunstwerk von Artisten, Tänzerinnen und Perfor-
mancekünstlern – darunter ein tanzender Pierrot und
ein philosophierender Clown – eingebettet.

Die Veranstaltung selbst sowie die begleitenden Be-
richte und Reportagen in Zeitung, Funk und Fernsehen
machten deutlich, dass der Mainzer Karneval und mit
ihm der Mainzer Carneval-Verein fest zum kulturellen
Leben in der Region gehören.

The challenge facing performance designer and director
Enno-Ilka Uhde was combining traditional elements of
the Mainz Carnival campaign opening and those stipu-
lated by protocol with a modern presentation that incorporated performance aspects and outside artists.
The solution: to embed the entrance of the roughly 70
guards and the prince and princess, the official election
of the couple and the various speeches and laudations in
a synthesis of artistes, dancers and performance artists –
including a dancing Pierrot and a philosophizing clown.

The event itself, as well as the accompanying reports
and coverage in newspapers, on radio and television,
clearly showed that the Mainz Carnival and the Mainzer
Carneval-Verein are a firm part of the region's cultural
life.

Eigens für das Ereignis komponierte der englische Komponist Matt Clifford die Prinzenhymne, die der Mainzer Domchor, begleitet vom Industrial Brass Tentett, zum Einzug des Prinzenpaars vortrug.

British composer Matt Clifford composed the "Prince hymn" especially for the event, which was performed by the Mainz Cathedral Choir accompanied by the Industrial Brass Tentett during the entrance of the prince and princess.

**Agency** Industrial Theater, Karlsruhe **Client** Mainzer Carneval-Verein 1838 e.V., Mainz **Location** Palace of the Counts Elector, Mainz, Germany **Month / Year** November 2012 **Duration** One day **Concept / Dramaturgy / Direction / Coordination** Enno-Ilka Uhde – Performance-Designer and Regisseur, Industrial Theater, Karlsruhe **Graphics / Communication** Mainzer Carneval-Verein **Event technology** Flo Service GmbH, Andreas Hörig – Master of event technology, Mainz **Media** SWR; RTL; local radio stations, tv channels and print media **Artists** Nasly Deniz Boran; Pierre Wyss, Liubov Vitanova; Industrial Dancers, Ulla Bladin; Philippe Rives, Mister He, Cordula Münchmeyer; Golden Power of Hungary; Die Buschs; Matthias Hammerschmitt; Industrial Brass Tentett, Dirk Hirthe; Cathedral chorus of Mainz; Ministerals of Mainz; Thomas Neger; Die Konfettis, Gardists and carnival protagonists of Mainz **Decoration** Inspiration, Dieter P. Wenger, Mainz **Catering** Hilton Mainz **Photos** Tom Kohler, Karlsruhe

# DIAMANT. The Swiss Award for Journalism
## SceneDeluxe

Location: Bern Concert Theatre, Switzerland

Der Schweizer Medienpreis „Diamant" will die lokale Berichterstattung in der Schweiz fördern und pflegen. Lokaljournalisten arbeiten an der Basis – unter dieser Prämisse wurde der Schweizer Medienpreis 2012 konzipiert.

The Swiss award for journalism "Diamant" (Diamond), seeks to promote and cultivate local news coverage in Switzerland. Local journalists work at grass-roots level, and it was with this in mind that the Swiss media prize was conceived in 2012.

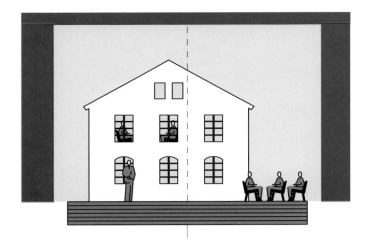

Nirgendwo kommen Journalisten und ihr Produkt so unmittelbar in Kontakt mit Lesern, Zuschauern und Zuhörern wie auf der lokalen Ebene. Lokaljournalisten erfüllen eine exklusive und zugleich wichtige Aufgabe: Sie berichten, beschreiben, fotografieren und untersuchen, was vor unserer Haustür geschieht. Deshalb gehört der Schweizer Medienpreis für Lokaljournalismus auf die Straße – mitten unter sein Publikum.

Hieran lehnte sich das Gesamtkonzept der Preisverleihung an. Die Bühne wurde als Platz mit einer typischen Schweizer Häuserkulisse angelegt. Fenster gaben den Blick in das Innere der Häuser frei, deren „Bewohner" Zeitungsleser, Fernsehzuschauer, Radiohörer und Online-User mimten. Die Szenerie wechselte zwischen Tag und Nacht; die Häuser und der Hintergrund veränderten mittels Videoprojektion und 3D-Mapping ihre Gestalt und den Standort. Musiker spielten auf der Straße, Passanten und Journalisten diskutierten, es wurden Fotos und eine Umfrage gemacht.

Die nominierten Arbeiten wurden ebenfalls auf den Häuserfassaden präsentiert. Hierfür wurde eine individuelle Bildsprache entwickelt, die sich an der Form und den Konturen der Kulissen orientierte.

Nowhere do journalists and their product come into such close contact with readers, listeners and viewers as at the local level. Local journalists do a job that is both exclusive and important: They report, describe, photograph and examine what happens on our doorsteps. This is why the Swiss award for journalism belongs on the street – surrounded by its audience.

This idea served as the basis for the concept behind the award's ceremony. The stage was modeled on a square with a backdrop of typical Swiss houses. Through the windows it was possible to see the "occupants" who mimicked people reading newspapers, watching TV, listening to the radio and surfing the Web. The scenery alternated between day and night; the houses and the background altered their guise and location thanks to video projections and 3D-mapping. Musicians played on the street, passers-by talked to journalists, photos were taken and a survey conducted.

The nominated works were likewise presented on the house façades. This was done using individual imagery that adapted to the shape and contours of the backdrop.

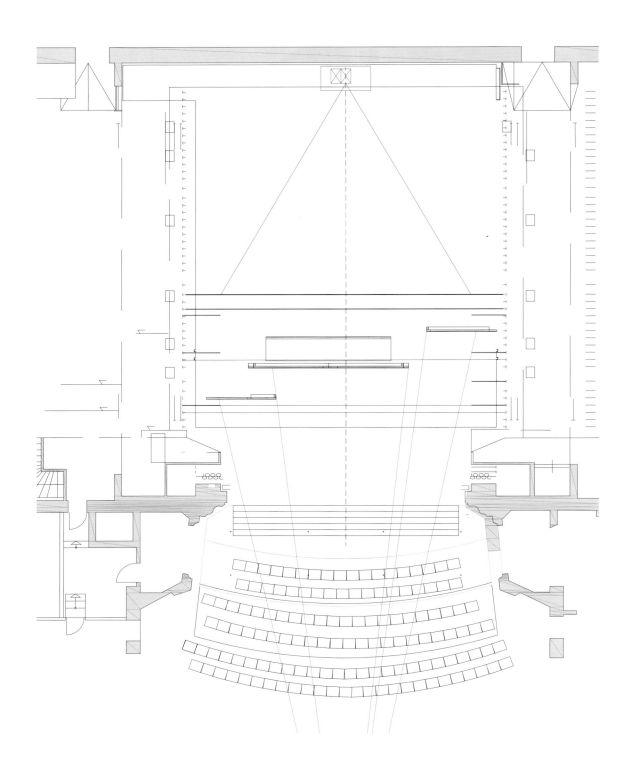

**Agency** SceneDeluxe GbR, Hamburg **Client** Fondation Reinhardt von Graffenried, Bern **Location** Konzert Theater Bern, Switzerland **Month/Year** April 2012 **Duration** One day **Concept/Dramaturgy stage programme/Decoration** SceneDeluxe **Direction/Coordination** Gunther Len Schönfeld, SceneDeluxe **Architecture** Andrea Bohacz, SceneDeluxe **Media** Visiontools GmbH **Lighting/Construction** Konzert Theater Bern **Films** eachfilm GmbH **Music** Jefim Jourist Quartett **Artists/Showacts** Mireille Jaton, Hans-Peter Müller-Drossart **Photos** Andy Tobler, Zurich

# Quartet
## LA FURA DELS BAUS

Location: Teatro alla Scala, Milan

Das Theaterstück „Quartett" von Heiner Müller, das auf dem Briefroman „Gefährliche Liebschaften" von Chorderlos de Laclos basiert, wurde 2011 für das Teatro alla Scala in Mailand von der katalanischen Theatergruppe La Fura dels Baus als Oper adaptiert.

In 2011, Heiner Müller's play "Quartet" which is based on the epistolary novel "Dangerous Liaisons" by Chorderlos de Laclos, was adapted as an opera for the Teatro alla Scala in Milan by the Catalan theater group La Fura dels Baus.

Heiner Müller reduzierte die aristokratische Staffage der literarischen Vorlage auf die zwei Hauptdarsteller Merteuil und Valmont, ein Paar mittleren Alters, das in einer westlichen Stadt völlig abgeschottet und isoliert von der äußeren Welt lebt. Hier verdichtet sich nun das Intrigenspiel der Geschlechter zu einem Zweikampf zwischen Frau und Mann um Macht, Kontrolle und Gewalt, der das Paar schließlich ins Verderben stürzt.

Ausgehend von der musikalischen Idee Luca Francesconis wurde die Oper auf drei räumlichen Ebenen aufgebaut. Die erste Ebene – „Inside" – präsentiert sich als trostloser und kalter Raum, ähnlich einem Bunker oder einer Zelle, in dem sich das intime Leben der Hauptdarsteller abspielt. Hingegen verbildlicht die Ebene „Outside" die mentale Welt von Merteuil und Valmont: Alles, was die beiden denken und fühlen, wird in diesem außenliegenden Raum sichtbar. Die Ebene „Out" ist schließlich als metaphysischer Raum zu verstehen, der außerhalb alles Menschlichen existiert und sich lediglich von den universalen Naturgesetzen dirigieren lässt.

Heiner Müller reduced the aristocratic window-dressing of the original novel to the two main protagonists Merteuil and Valmont, a middle-aged couple that lives in a western town totally isolated from the outside world. The intriguing between the sexes is condensed into a battle between man and woman about power, control and violence, which ultimately destroys the couple.

Taking the musical idea of Luca Francesconi as a starting point, the opera was composed around three spatial levels. The first level – "inside" – presents itself as a cold, miserable room similar to a bunker or a cell in which the intimate life of the main actors takes place. By contrast, the level "outside" visualizes the emotional world of Merteuil and Valmont: Everything that the two people think and feel is visible in this exterior space. Finally, the level "out" is to be understood as a metaphysical space, which exists outside of everything human and is controlled by the universal laws of nature alone.

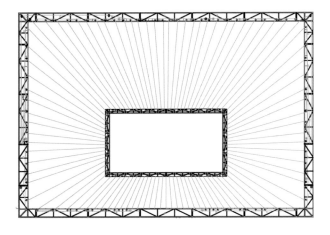

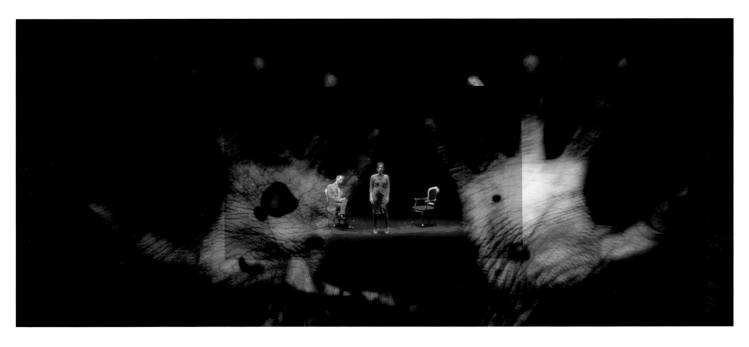

Dieses Konzept wurde auf der Bühne auch szeno-
grafisch umgesetzt. Das Hauptelement bildete ein
7x4x3,80 m großer Kasten, der in der Mitte des Rau-
mes schwebte und den Darstellern als Aktionsebene
diente. Außerhalb der Zelle wurden die Gefühle und
Gedanken der Figuren als Videoprojektionen verbildlicht und von Elementen aus der metaphysischen
Ebene „Out" umgeben. Die audiovisuelle Sprache von
„Quartett" ermöglichte es also, die physischen Gren-
zen der Szenerie aufzuheben sowie zwischen mikro-
und makroskopischer Perspektive zu wechseln.

This concept was also transferred to the scenography on
the stage. A large box suspended in the center of the
room served the actors as an action level and was the
main element. Outside of this cell the feelings and
thoughts of the figures were visualized as video projections and surrounded by elements from the metaphysical level "out". As such, the audiovisual language of
"Quartet" makes it possible to remove the physical di-
vides of the scenery but also to alternate between the
microscopic and macroscopic perspective.

**Agency** LA FURA DELS BAUS, Barcelona **Client** Teatro alla Scala, Milan **Location** Teatro alla Scala, Milan, Italy **Month / Year**
April 2011 **Duration** Several days **Concept and Artistic Direction** Àlex Ollé **Scenography** Alfons Flores **Lighting** Marco
Filibeck **Films** Franc Aleu **Music** Luca Francesconi **Costumes** Lluc Castells **Photos** Rudy Amisano, Teatro alla Scala
**Awards** Premio Abbiati at "La migliore Novità assoluta"

# Thinking of Germany – "How Do We (Not) Want to Live in the Future?"

## TRIAD Berlin

Location: Atrium of Deutsche Bank, Berlin, Germany

WAS NEHMEN SIE MIT?

Antwort: Frauenquote

Am 28. September 2012 fand das vierte Forum der Konferenzreihe „Denk ich an Deutschland" in Berlin statt. Unter der Leitfrage „Wie wollen wir in Zukunft (nicht) leben?" befasste sich die Konferenz mit der Zukunft der deutschen Nachhaltigkeitsindustrie und dem grünen Zukunftsoptimismus.

On September 28, 2012 the fourth forum of the conference series "Thinking of Germany" took place in Berlin. Guided by the main question "How do we (not) want to live in the future?" the conference addressed Germany's sustainability industry and green optimism about the future.

Weitere Themen wie die dunkle Seite der Macht von Algorithmen und Maschinen sowie die Frage, wie wir in Zukunft (nicht) leben möchten, wurden von den Teilnehmern diskutiert. Das Event genoss mediale Aufmerksamkeit – nicht zuletzt aufgrund seiner prominenten Redner: Harald Schmidt hielt die Eröffnungsrede und Bundeskanzlerin Dr. Angela Merkel gab in den Schlussworten eine Antwort auf die Frage „Wie wollen wir leben?"

Im historischen Atrium der Deutschen Bank in Berlin wurde für die Konferenz eine temporäre Architektur errichtet: ein Raum-in-Raum-Konzept, umgesetzt mit dem primären Gestaltungselement Umzugskartons, einem zentralen Paneltisch und einer großen LCD-Stegloswand. Die Kartons wurden mit Begriffen und Fragen aus dem Konferenzprogramm bedruckt. Die Frage „Was wollen Sie in die Zukunft mitnehmen?" lud die Teilnehmer zu Interaktion ein und regte weiterführenden Diskussionen an.

Participants also discussed other topics such as the dark side of the power of algorithms and machines, and the question of how do we (not) want to live in the future. The event enjoyed considerable media coverage, not least of all thanks to its renowned speakers: Harald Schmidt delivered the opening speech and in the closing remarks, the German Chancellor Dr. Angela Merkel provided an answer to the question "How do we want to live?".

In the historical atrium of the Deutsche Bank in Berlin a temporary architecture was installed for the conference, a "room within a room" concept, realized using packing cases as the primary design element, a central panel table and a large seamless LCD wall. The cases were printed with terms and questions from the conference program. The question "What do you want to take with you to the future" invited participants to interact, and inspired further discussions.

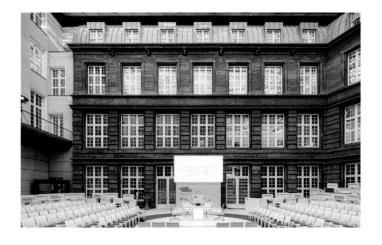

Die Konferenzarchitektur spiegelte die Konferenzinhalte Partizipation und Nachhaltigkeit wider. So entstand die passende Atmosphäre, um Fragen zu gesellschaftlichen und sozialen Innovationen sowie nach Orientierung der internationalen Politik in Krisenzeiten zu diskutieren.

The conference architecture reflected the conference topics of participation and sustainability. This created a fitting atmosphere for discussing questions about societal and social innovations, but also the orientation of international politics in times of crisis.

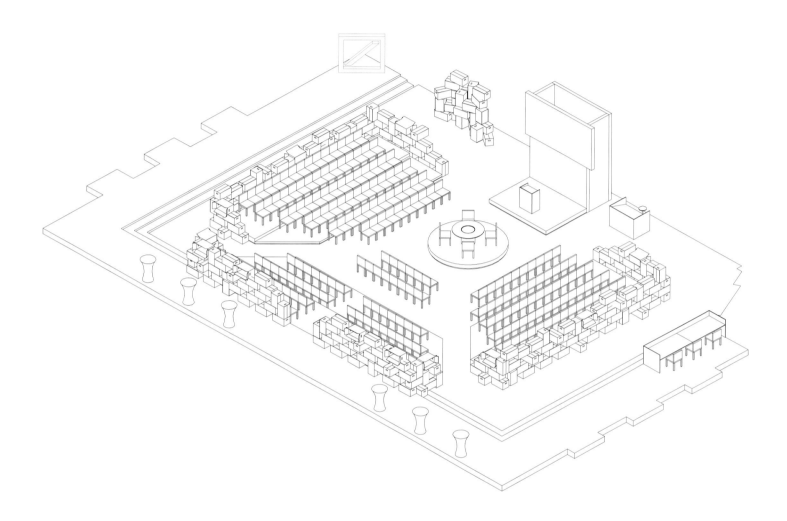

**Agency** TRIAD Berlin Projektgesellschaft mbH, Berlin **Client** Alfred Herrhausen Society – The international Forum of Deutsche Bank mbH, Berlin **Location** Atrium of Deutsche Bank, Berlin, Germany **Month / Year** September 2012 **Duration** One day **Concept / Dramaturgy / Direction / Coordination / Architecture / Graphics / Communication / Media / Films** TRIAD **Lighting** Neumann & Müller GmbH **Decoration** Delafair GmbH, qunic GmbH **Catering** Alois Dallmayr KG **Construction** Delafair **Photos** Frank Rösner, Berlin

# Henri Nannen Award 2012
## SceneDeluxe

Location: Deutsches Schauspielhaus Hamburg, Germany

Die Inszenierung des Henri Nannen Preises wurde 2012 als Symbiose aus Theater und Event gestaltet. Der Preis soll das Andenken des Stern-Gründers Henri Nannen lebendig halten und den Qualitätsjournalismus im deutschsprachigen Raum fördern.

The presentation of the Henri Nannen Award 2012 was conceived as a synthesis of theater and event. The award is intended to keep alive the memory of the founder of "Stern" magazine, Henri Nannen, and promote high-quality journalism in Germany, Switzerland and Austria.

Passend zum Konzept der Theaterinszenierung wurden die Preisverleihungen in den verschiedenen journalistischen Kategorien in hinführende Musik-, Schauspiel- und Kabarettszenen eingebettet.

Die über 1.000 Gäste aus Kultur, Medien, Politik und Wirtschaft wurden mit einer großen Lounge überrascht: Die „Guckkastenarchitektur" des über 100 Jahre alten Hamburger Schauspielhauses wurde aufgebrochen, indem Bühne und Zuschauersaal zu einem einzigen Raum verschwammen. Das Kernstück bildete ein Rundscreen über einer Bar. Dieser maß im Durchmesser 4 m und wurde im Verlauf der Inszenierung wiederholt zum Spielort journalistischer Dialoge. Der schwebende Zylinder war in Form und Funktion eine Reminiszenz an die klassischen Druckmedien und schlug durch die auf den Zylinder rotierend projizierten Inhalte eine Brücke in die Gegenwart.

In keeping with the theater setting the presentation ceremony in the various journalistic categories was embedded in suitable music, theater and cabaret scenes.

Over 1,000 guests from culture, media, politics and business were surprised to find themselves in a large lounge: Stage and auditorium merged to form a single room replacing the "proscenium architecture" of the Hamburg Schauspielhaus, which is over 100 years old. The centerpiece was a round screen above a bar measuring four meters in diameter. In the course of the event, it was repeatedly used for journalistic dialogs. In form and function the suspended cylinder recalled classic print media, and through the rotating content projected onto the cylinder forged a link to the present day.

Das gesamte Schauspielhaus wurde für den Henri Nannen Preis „umgebaut": Empfang und Garderoben wurden vor das Haus verlagert, die Garderobenausgaben im Haus wurden zu Büffetstationen und Bars, gekocht wurde in einem Zelt auf der Straße. Stuhlreihen wurden im Theatersaal nach der Verleihung aus- und Bars für die Aftershow-Party eingebaut.

The theater underwent a complete transformation for the Henri Nannen Award: lobby and cloakrooms were moved to the front of the building, while cloakroom counters became buffet areas and bars, with food being cooked in a tent on the road. After the presentation ceremony rows of chairs were removed from the theater and bars were installed for the after show party.

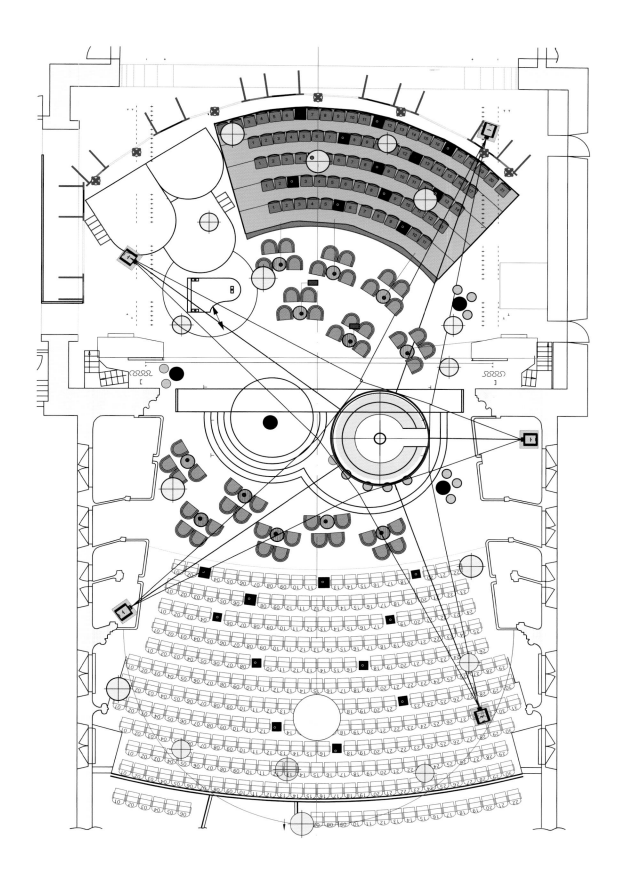

**Agency** SceneDeluxe GbR, Hamburg **Client** Gruner+Jahr / stern Projektbüro, Hamburg **Location** Deutsches Schauspiel-haus Hamburg, Germany **Month / Year** May 2012 **Duration** One day **Concept / Dramaturgy stage programme** SceneDe-luxe, stern Projektbüro **Direction / Coordination** Gunther Len Schönfeld, SceneDeluxe **Architecture** Andrea Bohacz, SceneDeluxe **Graphics / Communication** Kaluza+Schmid GmbH **Media** Visiontools GmbH **Lighting** Gunther Hecker GmbH **Films** eachfilm GmbH **Music** Matthias Stötzel **Artists / Showacts** Jamie Cullum, Soulisten, Judith Rakers, Hans Jochen Wagner, Chin Meyer **Decoration stage** SceneDeluxe **Decoration house** Kaluza+Schmid GmbH **Catering** Hotel Atlantic Kempinski Hamburg **Construction** Studio Hamburg Media Consult International (MCI) GmbH **Photos** Peter Lund, Ham-burg (eachfilm GmbH); Tom Borgmann, Hamburg (Visiontools GmbH)

# "Aktion Mensch moves" - City Tour 2012
## insglück

Location: Several locations in Germany

**AKTION MENSCH**

Mit ihrer bundesweiten Städtetour 2012 machte die Aktion Mensch Inklusion - das selbstverständliche Miteinander von Menschen mit und ohne Behinderung - erlebbar, indem sie die Menschen zum Tanzen brachte.

With its nationwide city tour in 2012, "Aktion Mensch" enabled people to experience inclusion - the natural coexistence of people with and without disabilities - by getting them to dance.

Alle Besucher waren eingeladen, sich hinter einer überdimensionalen Schablone des neuen Aktion-Mensch-Logos zu bewegen und damit Teil des ersten „inklusiven Musikvideos" zum Lied „Wunder" von Andreas Bourani zu werden.

Bei der Tour präsentierte die Aktion Mensch ihr neues Corporate Design erstmals in der Öffentlichkeit: Es stellt deutlicher und emotionaler als bisher das Ziel einer inklusiven Gesellschaft in den Mittelpunkt und macht die Arbeit der Aktion Mensch transparent. Das zentrale Element des neuen Corporate Designs ist das flexible Logo, das mit individuellen Motiven befüllt werden kann. Es rückt Menschen und Projekte, die mit der Aktion Mensch zusammen etwas bewegen, in den Mittelpunkt. Das neue Logo verdeutlicht so den Markenkern „Gemeinsam Chancen schaffen" und ist das Resultat der geschärften Markenpositionierung.

All visitors were invited to dance behind a larger-than-life template of the new "Aktion Mensch" logo, and become part of the first inclusion music video to the song "Wunder" (Miracle) by Andreas Bourani.

During the tour "Aktion Mensch" presented its new corporate design to the public for the first time: More clearly and more emotionally than before, it places the emphasis on working towards an inclusive society, and visualizes the work "Aktion Mensch" does. The key element of the new corporate design is the flexible logo, which can be filled with individual content. It shifts the focus firmly to the people and projects, that together with "Aktion Mensch" get things moving. As such, the new logo, the result of clearer brand positioning, clearly spells out the brand core "creating opportunities together".

Das Ziel der Städtetour, bundesweit noch mehr Aufmerksamkeit für das Kernthema der Aktion Mensch, Inklusion, zu schaffen, wurde durch den neuen Markenauftritt unterstützt. Das gemeinsame Erlebnis über alle Unterschiede hinweg zeigte, worauf es der Aktion Mensch ankommt: Vielfalt als Bereicherung für die Gesellschaft zu vermitteln.

Die Aktion Mensch will das Thema Inklusion mit Aktionen und Kampagnen sowie mit ihrer Projektförderung in der Gesellschaft voranbringen. Sie setzt sich dafür ein, dass Menschen mit und ohne Behinderung gleichberechtigt an allen gesellschaftlichen Prozessen teilhaben und selbstbestimmt leben können.

The new brand image supported the objective of the city tour, to raise awareness throughout Germany for the core topic of Aktion Mensch, namely, inclusion. Being able to experience something together, despite all the differences, demonstrated what "Aktion Mensch" is all about: communicating diversity as an enrichment for society.

With its actions and campaigns, as well as by promoting various projects, "Aktion Mensch" seeks to advance inclusion in society. It is devoted to ensuring that people with and without disabilities can participate equally in all societal processes and can live independent lives.

**Agency** insglück Gesellschaft für Markeninszenierungen mbH, Berlin **Client** Aktion Mensch e. V., Bonn **Location** Munich, Nuremberg, Erfurt, Dresden, Leipzig, Berlin, Hamburg, Bremen, Hannover, Dortmund, Düsseldorf, Stuttgart, Frankfurt/ Main, Cologne, Bonn, Germany **Month/Year** August–October 2012 **Duration** Six weeks **Concept/Dramaturgy/Direction/Coordination/Graphics/Communication** insglück **Music** Andreas Bourani **Artists/Showacts** Lisa Ulrich, Gebärden-Dolmetscherin **Photos** Kolja Matzke

# Nachwuchs in der Live-Kommunikation – Zwischen Generation Y und fehlender Ausbildung

FAMAB Verband Direkte Wirtschaftskommunikation e.V.

Es klingt nach einer Mammutaufgabe, denn der Branche geht der Nachwuchs aus. War es noch vor fünf Jahren üblich, dass sich im Monat rund 250 Absolventen bei einer durchschnittlich bekannten Eventagentur beworben haben, herrscht heute in den Eingangskörbchen der Personaler Ebbe. Die Gründe hierfür sind vielschichtig: Viele Berufseinsteiger setzen beim ersten Job auf klangvolle Namen oder „sexy" Branchen und gehen damit der direkten Wirtschaftskommunikation verloren. Die Crux dabei ist, dass sie schon nach kurzer Zeit gelangweilt, genervt und mit ihrem aktuellen Job unzufrieden sind. Zu diesem Ergebnis kommt das renommierte Marktforschungsinstitut trendence in seiner jährlichen Studie „Young Professional Barometer". Ein Viertel der Befragten fühlt sich unterfordert, 35 Prozent durch starre Strukturen ausgebremst. Besonders unzufrieden sind die Befragten mit dem Führungsstil ihres Unternehmens.

Auf der anderen Seite gibt es die Young Professionals, die den Weg in die direkte Wirtschaftskommunikation gefunden haben: Diese sind inhaltlich gefordert, in wechselnde Teams integriert und haben eine hohe Eigenverantwortung. Ist also alles in Butter für die Live-Kommunikation? – Leider nicht. Nach Meinung des FAMAB, dem führenden Verband der qualitätsgeprüften Spezialisten in der direkten Wirtschaftskommunikation, stellen sich zwar die Probleme von Unterforderung oder starren Strukturen in der Branche nicht, „trotzdem merken wir, dass die Anzahl der qualifizierten Absolventen, die eine Karriere in der Live-Kommunikation anstreben, nachlässt", resümiert Verbandsvize Jörn Huber. Immer wieder neue Herausforderungen, wechselnde Teams und flache Hierarchien – dafür steht die direkte Wirtschaftskommunikation. Sie steht aber auch für lange, projektbezogene Arbeitszeiten und relativ geringe Gehälter." Für eine Generation, die sich immer weniger über den Beruf definiert und neben dem Job auf genügend Raum für ein erfülltes Privatleben setzt, scheidet die Live-Kommunikation allein aufgrund der Stellenbeschreibung aus.

„Wenn wir auch in Zukunft für unsere Auftraggeber aus der Industrie erfolgreiche Marketingkonzepte umsetzen wollen, müssen wir die Attraktivität der Jobs steigern", so Huber. „Ein Faktor, mit dem wir sicherlich punkten können, sind flexible Arbeitszeiten." Zwar wird es in der Branche nur in Ausnahmefällen echte Halbtagsjobs geben, aber Homeoffice-Lösungen oder die Beschränkung auf wenige Projekte können bspw. für junge Eltern die Jobs attraktiver machen. Und bezüglich der geringeren Gehälter? – „Da müssen sich die Kunden unserer Mitglieder im Klaren sein, dass sie auf lange Sicht keine profilierten, erfahrenen Ansprechpartner mehr auf der anderen Seite des Tisches finden werden, wenn sie immer weiter an der Preisschraube drehen", weiß Verbandsgeschäftsführerin Elfie Adler.

Ein weiteres Problem sieht sie allerdings auch in der Tatsache, dass bei vielen Schul- und Hochschulabgängern die Branche nicht als potentieller Arbeitgeber angekommen ist. „Die Eröffnung der Olympischen Spiele, von Markenwelten wie der Autostadt in Wolfsburg sowie der weltgrößten Messen – all das gäbe es ohne die Spezialisten für Markenerlebnisse, Architektur und Begegnungen nicht," unterstreicht Adler.

Um der Tendenz der rückläufigen Bewerbungen entgegenzuwirken, hat der Verband bereits die ersten Schritte getan: Mit seinem Recruitment-Award DAVID richtet er sich an Abschlusssemester in Hochschulen, die im Rahmen eines Projekts anhand eines realen Briefings und in Zusammenarbeit mit einer Agentur zwei Konzepte entwickeln und diese einer hochkarätigen Jury vorstellen. So lernen die angehenden Young Professionals den Arbeitsalltag in einer Agentur kennen und können sich danach anhand von fundiertem Wissen für oder gegen die Branche entscheiden. „Und da punkten wir sehr häufig gegenüber den Hochglanzbroschüren, die namhafte Markenartikler auf Absolventenkongressen verteilen," weiß Jörn Huber.

Doch ein anderer Punkt ist tiefgreifender und besorgniserregender: Alle Absolventen, die ihr Hochschulstudium abschließen, sind Quereinsteiger in der direkten Wirtschaftskommunikation. Es fehlt der Branche immer noch eine fundierte Ausbildung im Bereich der Konzeption von Live-Kommunikation. Bisher stellt sich die Ausbildungssituation so dar, dass Hochschulen zwar Theater- und Kommunikationswissenschaftler, (Innen-)Architekten sowie Betriebswirte ausbilden, ein Ausbildungsgang für Kreation in der Live-Kommunikation aber fehlt. Das ist umso bedauerlicher, weil Veranstaltungen mit konkreten kommunikativen Zielen eine der komplexesten Herausforderungen im Marketingmix

von Unternehmen sind. Hier geht es um Dramaturgie und Vernetzung, um Unternehmensbotschaften, um Inszenierung im Sinne der Marke und darum, Emotionen beim Rezipienten hervorzurufen. Außerdem gilt es, die entsprechenden Inhalte zu vermitteln. Da ist es bspw. nicht ausreichend, als Theaterwissenschaftler die szenisch lineare Dramaturgie eines Aristoteles verinnerlicht zu haben.

„Wir sind uns bewusst, dass die gesamte Branche hier zusammenrücken und ihr Potential über Hochschul-, Verbands- und Kunden- bzw. Agenturgrenzen hinweg bündeln muss. Sonst wird sie mittelfristig dem Dilemma nicht entgehen können, dass Live-Kommunikation für das Unternehmensmarketing immer wichtiger wird, differenzierte Konzepte benötigt werden, es aber an Spezialisten fehlt, die solche Konzepte entwickeln und beurteilen können," so Huber. Hier findet sich das Potential für herausfordernde Tätigkeiten, die weit mehr sind als ein Job.

Es bleibt also spannend in der Live-Kommunikation und deshalb ist diese Branche auch ein adäquater Arbeitgeber für eine Generation, die nicht mit einem Fahrzeug, sondern mit einem Fragezeichen in Verbindung gebracht wird. Es muss ihr nur mal jemand sagen!

www.famab.de    www.eva-award.de

# Young professionals in live communications – Between Generation Y and a knowledge gap

FAMAB Verband Direkte Wirtschaftskommunikation e.V.

It sounds like a mammoth task indeed, for the sector is running out of young talent. Whereas only five years ago around 250 graduates a month would typically apply to an averagely well-known event agency, today the applications are only trickling into the HR inboxes. There are various reasons for this state of affairs: Many career entrants look to land their first job at renowned companies or in "sexy" industries and are thus lost to direct business communications. The crux of the matter is that they quickly get bored, annoyed and dissatisfied with their job. These are the findings presented by the renowned market research institute trendence in its annual study "Young Professional Barometer". One quarter of those surveyed felt they were not being sufficiently challenged, and 35 percent saw themselves as being held back by rigid structures. Respondents were particularly dissatisfied with their company's style of management.

On the other side are the young professionals who have found their way into direct business communication. They are challenged at work, integrated into alternating teams and have a high degree of personal responsibility. So is everything hunky-dory for live communications? – Unfortunately not. According to the FAMAB, the leading association of quality-approved specialists in direct business communications, there are no problems with rigid structures or insufficiently challenging work in the sector, "but nonetheless we are seeing a drop in the number of qualified graduates aspiring to a career in live communications", says association Deputy Jörn Huber in summary. "Ever new challenges, alternating teams and flat hierarchies – that is what direct business communications

stands for. Yet it also stands for long, project-based working hours and relatively low pay." For a generation that is less and less defined by profession and for which a fulfilling private life alongside their job is important, live communications falls at the first hurdle, namely the job description.

"If we want to realize successful marketing concepts for our clients in the industry in the future too, we have to make jobs more attractive", notes Huber. "One factor that is a definite plus is flexible working hours." Although actual part-time jobs are very rare in the sector, working from home or limiting oneself to just a few projects can make jobs more attractive, e.g., for young parents. And the low salaries? – "Our members' clients simply need to be aware that in the long term they will not be able to have established, experienced people on the other side of the table if they continue to keep pushing the price down", says Managing Director of the association Elfie Adler.

She also sees a problem in the fact that many school and college graduates do not perceive the sector as a potential employer. "The opening of the Olympic Games, "brand worlds" like Autostadt in Wolfsburg and the major international trade fairs – none of these would exist without the specialists in brand experience, architecture and interaction," emphasizes Adler.

The association has already taken initial steps to counteract the trend of falling applications. Its recruitment award DAVID is geared towards final-semester university students, who are to develop and present to an expert jury two concepts within the framework of a project with a real brief and in cooperation with an agency. In this way the aspiring young professionals get to know what daily working life is like at an agency and can make an informed decision about whether the sector is for them. "And that's where we often have an advantage over the glossy brochures distributed by renowned brand companies at graduate conventions," states Jörn Huber.

Yet there is another matter that is deeper-seated and more worrisome. All university graduates enter direct business communications from another discipline. The sector still does not have a solid training program in the area of live communications and its conceptualization. Although universities offer courses in Theater and Communication Studies, Interior Design and Architecture and Business Administration, there is no program for creative concepts in live communications. This is a regrettable state of affairs, especially given that events with specific communicative goals are one of the most complex challenges in a company's marketing mix. They involve dramaturgy and networking, company messages, staging the brand and eliciting an emotional response in observers. Moreover, the relevant information needs to be conveyed. Here graduates in Theater Studies, for instance, will find it is not enough to have learnt Aristotle's linear dramaturgy.

"We are aware that the entire sector needs to join together here and bundle its potential beyond the university, association and client/agency context. Otherwise in the medium term it won't be able to avoid the dilemma that live communications is becoming increasingly important for corporate marketing and tailored concepts are needed, but

there is a dearth of specialists able to develop and evaluate such concepts," says Huber. This is where the potential lies for challenging activities that are far more than just a job.

Thus, live communications remains an exciting field and as such this industry is also an appropriate employer for a generation still looking for direction and simply waiting for someone to point the way!

www.famab.de            www.eva-award.de

 FAMAB             EVA AWARD

# Impressum und Bildnachweise
# Imprint and credits

**Redaktion**
Editing               Christine Pfirrmann, Cornelia Reinhardt, Björn Stratmann

**Übersetzung**
Translations       Jeremy Gaines

**Gestaltungskonzept**
Design concept    **av**communication GmbH: Markus Mögel, Sandra Kessler

**Layout-Umsetzung**
Realisation         Christine Pfirrmann, Cornelia Reinhardt

**Coverfoto**
Cover photo       ACCIONA PRODUCCIONES Y DISEÑO (Events), Madrid

**Fotos Zäsurseiten**
Photos divider pages    8 f.    Andreas Keller, Altdorf
                        70 f.  diephotodesigner.de OHG, Berlin
                        94 f.  Ralf Rühmeier, Berlin
                        124f.  Andreas Keller, Altdorf
                        152 f.  ACCIONA PRODUCCIONES Y DISEÑO (Events), Madrid

**Lithografie**
Lithography        corinna rieber prepress, Marbach / Neckar

**Druck**
Printing            Leibfarth + Schwarz GmbH & Co. KG, Dettingen / Erms

**Papier**
Paper               ProfiSilk, 150g / m$^2$

ISBN 978-3-89986-181-5
Printed in Germany